So— What's for Dinner?

May 1993

PASTA FANTASIA

PASTA FANTASIA

Classic Italian Pasta Sauce Recipes

JANICE GIAMPA

Illustrated by Frank Westerberg

PEREGRINE PRESS, Publishers

Old Saybrook, Connecticut

This book is for my father

Designed by Frank Westerberg

Manufactured in the United States of America

First Printing

ACKNOWLEDGEMENTS

Having logged many hours writing this book, I have reached the point where I am quite relieved to see the finished product. But looking back on all those hours of collecting and cataloguing recipes, testing and retesting sauces, travelling and translating, writing and rewriting, I honestly cannot say that it has been difficult work. In truth, I have had a grand time, enjoying every minute spent on a labor of love. Much of the pleasure I got from writing this book came from the many friends and acquaintances, both here and abroad, who I visited and who generously donated their time and expertise. The book could not have been completed without them. So, in traditional fashion, I would like to acknowledge them here.

Thanks go to the fine Italian cooks who aided me in my search for authentic regional specialties. They include Maria A. Giampa from Roma; Lola Grillo from Marzano Appia in Campania; Rossella Menchinella from Acquacanina in Marche; Alida Lemucchi from Montorio Al Vomano in Abruzzo; Carmela Puntillo from Cinquefronde, Calabria; Cetti D'Ambra from Napoli; and Silvia Marchese from Palermo, Sicilia. Special thanks are also due Alfredo Di Lelio in Roma, the grandson of the original "Alfredo" (as in Fettuccine all'Alfredo), for giving me his family's famous recipe and notes and anecdotes on pasta sauces, as well as Dott. Carlo Mora, Molini e Pastifici Voiello, for giving me a tour of the Voiello pasta factory in Italy and for patiently answering all my questions. Grazie a tutti.

Domestically, thanks go to Marcia Tedone Grzybowski and Lorraine Giampa for their culinary contributions, and to Susan Heinrich for her help in preparing the manuscript. Special mention is due David Tedone, my husband, for his support throughout the project and specifically for traipsing around Italy with me (though he loved every minute of it!). Moreover, this book owes plenty to the skill, talent, and enthusiasm of Barry and Susan Hildebrandt, publishers, and to Frank Westerberg, who created the masterful drawings that bring this book to life.

TABLE OF CONTENTS

Vegetables with Meat and/or Seafood

Meat

Seafood

Quick Fixes

Salads

PASTA
FANTASIA

Pasta Fantasia

"*A tavola non s'invecchia*" is a Tuscan proverb that best describes the way Italians feel about dining: "One doesn't age at the table."

Preparing fresh vegetables, savoring a hearty meal, conversing with family and close friends, are simple acts of celebration from another age. In our world of supermarkets, fast-food restaurants, and 24-hour diners, it is hard to believe that peasants once spent their lives in the rugged Tuscan hills, coaxing a few crops: barley, wheat, olives, grapes, ghourds, figs, and herbs. These *fruits of labor* were their sole reward, which they no doubt ate with gusto at meal time—the only leisure they knew. Today, Italians still attach a special significance to *il pasto*. They will not be hurried while they eat, and they will enjoy it, explaining with aplomb, as custom dictates, that "time stands still when you enjoy a fine dinner."

When it comes to cooking, I like to keep the old idea of celebration in mind and approach a recipe playfully, the way Italians do. In fact, as history tells us, many pasta recipes were invented specifically to celebrate prized crops, whether they were eggplant, basil, tomatoes, capers, or peppers. Unfortunately, many cookbook writers treat pasta recipes like mathematical formulas; they translate the Italian penchant for the perfect ingredient into a dogmatic approach to cooking. Nothing could be further off the mark, because Italian recipes are often inexact and invite interpretation, particularly if the garden produces an exceptional crop of peppers, cauliflower, or whatever. A sauce should be determined by the pick of the day at the market, not by thumbing through a catalogue. With imagination and flair, you can create a sauce from almost any ingredient. As my father says, "To cook Italian, you have to be both a realist and a dreamer."

If you want to cook pasta, then, you have to be prepared to have some fun, because the playfulness in Italian cooking can even be seen in the names of recipes. For example, *Spaghetti alla puttanesca*, which refers to harlots, is so named because it is a spicey, alluring dish. *Mari e monte*, or pasta of the sea and mountains, poetically combines clams and mushrooms. And *Spaghetti alla carbonara*, which was originally made with lots of black pepper, takes it name from the coal miners of Southern Italy. The names of specific pasta shapes include *vermicelli* or "worms," *orecchiette* or "ears," and *strangolopreti* which means "that which strangles priests," and there are many others that raise an eyebrow or a chuckle.

The variety of pasta recipes could only have been achieved over time, as a product of history. Haunting recipes have been made from the most unexpected ingredients, such as pumpkin, squid, lemon rinds, and eggplant. And they can be based in olive oil, butter, cream, or sparkling wine. Some sauces are served for the main course; others are served for the first course, and still others are considered snacks or light lunches. The pasta itself comes in two basic varieties: long ribbons and short tubes. And yet, several hundred specific designs have been invented.

Italian pasta sauces are also the product of different regions with distinct crops, specialties, and culinary preferences. As a result, if viewed together, the canon of pasta recipes is eclectic. The sauces may be simple or complex, strong or delicate, rich or spare, sharp or mild, fancy or basic. Many have fascinating origins that are part fact, part fiction, but all reflect the imagination, or *fantasia*, of the people that produced them.

Pasta fantasia, the title of this book, refers to the most important ingredient in pasta sauces—imagination. The best sauces are filled with wit and flair, and communicate the spirit or disposition of the cook. Who cannot taste a breezy summer's day in *pesto*, or the passion and temper in *penne all'arrabiata*?

Moreover, no two cooks will ever produce the same pasta sauce, even if they use the same recipe. The subtle differences in ingredients, utensils, cooking techniques, and even the personalities and preferences of the cooks, inevitably come through. Each sauce reveals the fingerprint and identity of the cook.

I have tried, therefore, to collect a variety of pasta sauce recipes that anyone can make. The recipes contained in this book are all quick sauces that can be made, for the most part, in a skillet. Some recipes are classics; some are novelties, and some are my inventions, but all have a special, unmistakable character. Let your taste be the judge, and your imagination be the guide.

The Great Pasta Revolution

America is undergoing another revolution—not in politics, lifestyles, or even fashion, but in eating. Pasta, which was once a blue-collar special, has begun to appear on the menus of the swankiest restaurants. And not just pasta in tomato sauce, *fettuccine all'Alfredo*, *spaghetti alle vongole*, and *spaghetti carbonara* (what I call the familiar four). The more exotic dishes, such as *pasta primavera*, *appasionata*, *cacio e pepe*, *mari e monte*, and *quattro formaggi*, are also becoming familiar, and even household names.

Interestingly enough, the pasta revolution was not set off by gourmets but by physical fitness buffs, who were concerned with nutrition. In fact, the nutritional value of pasta was first popularized by marathoners who practiced "carbo-bombing" before grueling races. The night before a race, they would load up on carbohydrates, primarily pasta and beer, to store the necessary

energy. Pasta quickly became the official food of marathoners, and synonymous with high energy.

But increased energy is not the only nutritional benefit from eating pasta. Medical reports have stressed the fact that Americans in general eat too many meats high in fats, and not enough grains and carbohydrates. Moreover, palatable substitutes for red meat are scarce. The fatty American diet leads to heart disease, and it has been linked to the high incidence of cancer. The Mediterranean diet, on the other hand, is relatively low in animal fats, and includes healthy portions of vegetables, fruit, olive oil, and pasta. Independent researchers in Europe and in the United States have concluded that the Mediterranean diet—where pasta figures prominantly—is better than the typical American diet.

Undoubtedly, the American economy has also helped renew interest in pasta. Italian pasta sauces may be the only palatable way that homemakers can stretch their food budgets. The ingredients in most pasta recipes cost much less than a hamburger dinner. In Italy, the per capita income is about $3,800 a year, while the per capita income in America is over $8,600 a year. Clearly, Italians have a greater incentive to eat pasta, because a diet rich in meats is expensive and excessive. But even the wealthiest Italians eat plenty of pasta. And in that pasta has been the national dish of Italy for centuries, a diet comprised largely of red meats would simply not satisfy the more sophisticated Italian palate. Pasta, nonetheless, remains true to its origins—it remains affordable. Pasta recipes reflect the Italians' ability to create delicacies from the most basic ingredients.

Ironically, the Italian diet, which costs less, is far more healthful than the "richer" American diet, which is largely responsible for the fattening of America. Americans, who eat on the average eleven pounds of pasta per person each year, generally weigh much more than Italians, who eat about seventy pounds of pasta per person per year. The idea that pasta is fattening is really a myth.

Pasta recipes are not only nutritious and inexpensive; they are also easy to make. Most recipes, even the most complex ones, can be made in the time it takes to boil a pot of water and cook a pound of pasta—say, 20 minutes. All the cook needs to do is sauté a few ingredients, and then let the sauce simmer long enough to bring out the full flavor. No fancy cooking techniques are required either; most recipes, once set on the stove, need occasional stirring, little else. Making a basic hollandaise sauce would be considered difficult when compared to the average pasta sauce. Even if you hate to cook, you will find that cooking pasta is fun and easy. Some sauces, like *burro e parmigiano* and *pesto*, require no cooking at all. And yet, Italian pasta recipes, made from inexpensive ingredients and prepared simply in minutes, will please the most discriminating gourmet.

You will have no trouble finding at least one recipe for every occasion. The wide range of Italian sauces reflects the abundance of produce in Italy. I have never tasted more delicious fruits and vegetables than those I ate in Italy. Cooks attribute the superb flavor to the soil and climate, and to the Italian farmer's know-how, because Italians take great pride in their vegetable gardens. Even Italians living in the congested neighborhoods of Rome, Milan, and Naples, have their tomato plants and boxes full of herbs. The Italian pride is reflected in the quality of all produce found at the market, and its influence can be felt in the simplest of pasta sauces.

PASTA:
THE BASIC
INGREDIENTS

Pasta:

Italians are not satisfied with the legend that an Italian, namely Marco Polo, first introduced pasta to the western world. Pasta, as any Italian knows, was invented in Italy long before Marco Polo made his famous journey to the Orient.

Many historians and food lovers have claimed evidence for the early existence of pasta in sources such as *The Decameron* of Boccaccio, which is said to mention *ravioli*, or in writings of Cicero, which refer to *lagunum*, a noodle eaten in the glory days of Rome. If historical controversies intrigue you, then you may be interested to know that Pontedassio, Italy, a city near Genoa, has a Spaghetti Museum that features all types of pasta memorabilia. The exhibits include various manuscripts on pasta and several types of tools and machines for making pasta that date back to ancient times.

Recently, a researcher in Genoa uncovered a document, dated February 2, 1279, that refers specifically to a "cask of dry pasta." The document turned out to be a will recorded by a Genovese notary concerning the estate of a deceased military commander. The official reference to pasta, most notably "dry" pasta, predates Marco Polo's return to Italy by some fifteen years.

Still, others less taken by the Italian evidence feel that the invention of pasta probably occurred several times over in several different locations. They suggest that pasta has been part of the national diet of many countries for several centuries. And, given its basic ingredients of flour and water, pasta (like bread) could have been invented almost anywhere in the world where grains were eaten.

In the United States, pasta was first introduced in the 1700s by none other than Thomas Jefferson who, as ambassador to France, had occasion to travel extensively throughout Italy. In fact, Jefferson tried to promote pasta in America, but it never caught on enough to become part of early American culture, except perhaps in the song "Yankee Doodle." You know, "Yankee Doodle stuck a feather in his hat and called it *macaroni*." Historians believe that the reference to macaroni

The Basic Ingredients

in "Yankee Doodle" poked fun at American aristocrats, who had adopted the avant garde practice of eating macaroni, also known as pasta.

Pasta really caught on in the United States in the late 1800s and early 1900s, when large populations of Europeans emigrated to America. This was particularly true when the Italian *mezzogiorno* was in full swing, and people from southern Italy began to arive at Ellis Island, New York, at a rate of more than five thousand a day. Today in America, when Italian cooking is mentioned, most people think of Southern Italian cooking, predominately tomato sauces, pizza, and olive oil—a legacy I suppose of the *mezzogiorno*. Despite their great popularity, the pasta dishes known throughout the United States are barely representative of the variety of Italian pasta dishes.

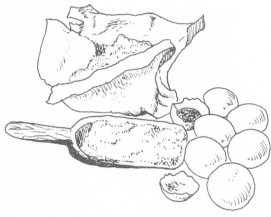

Pasta simply means paste, or more specifically a mixture of flour and water (and sometimes egg). In this book, I have concentrated on two main types of pasta: *asciutta* and *all'uova*.

Pasta *asciutta* is most familiar to Americans; it is "dry" pasta, or the type sold in most grocery stores. A number of fine American commercial brands can be purchased, but I have always favored the Italian imports. Most pasta is made with only flour and water (and a little elbow grease), but when eggs are added the pasta comes out softer. Pasta *all'uova*, or egg noodles, is typically made at home (what Italians call *fatta in casa*, or pasta *casalinga*) because it is easier to knead and roll than pasta made without eggs. The difference

in taste is far less noticeable than the difference in texture. However, pasta *all'uova* does not have to be soft either; it can be dried and kept for months.

Italians use a few other terms to differentiate the types of pasta. Pasta *ripieni* refers to any pasta that is stuffed, whether with cheese, meat, spinach, or herbs. Americans know pasta *ripieni* as lasagna, ravioli, manicotti, and stuffed shells. Pasta *in brodo* literally means pasta *in broth*, and it refers to any pasta, like pastine or stelle, used in soups. And pasta *al forno* refers to any pasta, such as the casserole version of gnocchi, that is baked in an oven.

Specific recipes call for different types of pasta. For example, in Emilia-Romagna, they use only a soft egg pasta with a heavy, full-bodied tomato sauce such as *Ragu alla Bolognese*. The texture of pasta has much to do with the ultimate flavor of the recipe. Even though the ingredients for pasta are quite basic, the technique for making and cooking it, as well as its shape, play an important role in Italian cooking. The recipes that I have included mainly call for pasta *asciutta*, although some do require pasta *all'uova*, and other recipes can use either effectively. Pasta *ripieni*, pasta *in brodo*, and pasta *al forno* are really quite different subjects and deserve separate volumes.

Pasta also comes in colors: green, pink, violet, brown, and tan, to name a few. But color, if not a basic property of the original flour, adds little to the flavor of the pasta itself. Colors are largely a touch of fancy. Most Italian food lovers are familiar with green pasta, which is made by adding finely chopped spinach to the pasta dough. (The traditional recipe calling for green pasta is *Paglio e fieno*, or straw and hay, referring to the green and yellow colors of the two pastas used in the dish.) Pink pasta is made by adding a little beet juice or chopped tomatoes, and violet pasta is created by adding minced beets. Whole wheat grain, which lately has become popular in the United States, can produce brown pasta, but the most novel is tan pasta. It is made by adding powdered cocoa to the pasta dough—it does little, if anything, for the taste.

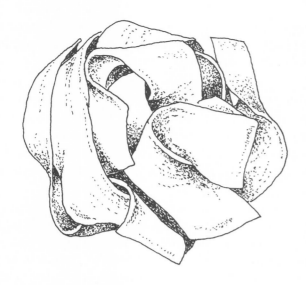

Pasta Designs

Mountains, regions, dialects, climates, customs, and politics divide the Italian people. But few things divide Italians like the preferred shape of pasta. Literally hundreds of designs have been invented, and they are served faithfully by cooks from Lombardia to Sicilia. In fact, the variety reflects the *fantasia* of pasta, because imagination abounds when it comes to the shape of pasta. Some look like butterflies, ribbons, tubes, beads, stars, dots, wheels, and even ears; they have musical names like *capelli, bucatini, fusilli, vermicelli, linguine*. Many shapes are so closely identified with geographical areas that ordering a different pasta in a local restaurant is grounds for suspicion.

The design of pasta is important when it comes to preparing the perfect dish. If you remember only one thing about pasta shapes, it should be this: *The design of pasta must complement the sauce*. A long, thin pasta such as *capelli* or *vermicelli* should be used with delicately flavored and light sauces. If a thick *penne* or *bucatini* is used with a light sauce, the pasta would dominate the serving. In addition, a long, smooth pasta is preferred for oil-based sauces. Smooth pasta is easily coated and yet is allows the excess oil to drain off into the plate. Thick pastas like *conchiglie* or *ziti*, which often have ridges, should not be used with an oil-based sauce. They are designed specifically to hold the sauce.

A thick pasta should be served with a hearty sauce that can stand up to it. The tubular designs like *rigatoni* or *tortiglioni*, with their fluted edges and ridges, are well-suited for heavy sauces. A thin pasta in a heavy sauce will not only fail to hold the flavoring and substance of the sauce, but it will also become difficult to eat.

By paying careful attention to the designs of pasta, you can easily tell which ones are best suited for particular recipes. In enough time, you may even begin to understand the method behind the Italian mania of creating so many different pasta shapes.

Macaroni and *spaghetti* are two words for pasta used in America that I feel need some clarification. The words are often used interchangeably; *macaroni* means any type of short, tubular or round pasta (presumably like ziti or conchiglie), while *spaghetti* refers to long, thin pasta. In Italy, macaroni (spelled *maccheroni*) is also used as a generic term, but spaghetti refers to a specific long, thin pasta that is a cousin to vermicelli and linguine. There is even a *spaghettini*, or little spaghetti, pasta which is simply a thinner version of spaghetti.

The catalogue of pasta is endless, and every time I find a new list or visit an Italian grocery store, I seem to discover another shape with an interesting story or two behind its origin. Many of those stories are fact and many no doubt are fiction, but they are always rather clever and somewhat amusing. Some pasta shapes like *fettuccine* are ancient, while others like *tagliatelle* have more recent and specific origins. Fettuccine is said to be a direct descendant of the Roman noodle *lagunum*, and tagliatelle was supposed to have been inspired by the golden locks of Lucrezia Borgia. (In truth, fettuccine and tagliatelle are quite similar, and few people can tell them apart.) Still, the origins of other designs, like the literal meanings of some pasta names, have been lost to antiquity.

The list I have provided is by no means exhaustive, but it does give a respectable sampling of pasta shapes, and you will be able to find at least one for every recipe and for every occasion.

Agnolotti. A round doughy pasta, usually stuffed with a mixture of ham or cheese and spices, and then folded. Agnolotti, which literally means "fat little lambs," are similar to ravioli.

Bucatini. A long, tubular pasta that resembles a soda straw. "Buca" means "hole" and no doubt refers to the hole in the center.

Capelli. The name of this pasta means "hair." And, as you might expect, this pasta is long and thin. A variation is called *capelli d'angelo*, or angel's hair; it is even thinner than capelli and comes wrapped like a nest.

Cappeletti. Translates into "little hats"; a doughy pasta stuffed with a mixture of ham or cheese and spices which resembles ravioli.

Cavatelli. A short, oblong macaroni with a hollow center; the name probably comes from the word *cavatura*, which means hollow.

Conchiglie. Familiar to most Americans as "shells," conchiglie literally means conch shells. It comes in several sizes, from the large *conchiglioni*, which are usually stuffed with ricotta cheese, to the small *conchigliette*.

Ditali. A small, tubular macaroni that resembles a "sewing thimble"—which is what its name means. It comes in several sizes; the smallest version is called *ditalini*.

Eliche. A short, ribbon-like pasta, characterized by its spiral shape. The name literally means "helix" or "spiral."

Farfalle. Literally translates into "butterflies," and this light pasta lives up to its name. The large size is known as *farfalloni*; the small size is called *farfalline*.

Fettuccine. Familiar to most pasta lovers, even in America. A long, flat noodle, often made with eggs and flour, the name literally means "tape." Fettuccine is a direct descendant of the ancient Roman noodle *lagunum*.

Fusilli. A long, spiral-shaped pasta that resembles a cork-screw. The name means "little spindles."

Gnocchi. In some dialects, "gnocchi" is slang for "blockhead," which I suppose could reflect the thick, doughy nature of gnocchi made with potatoes or ricotta cheese. Most people call it a dumpling. Another type of pasta, which is similar to conchiglie, is called *roman gnocchi*.

Lingue di Passero. The name means "sparrow tongues"; a short version of linguine, only a little flatter and somewhat thinner.

Linguine. A well-known pasta, long and thin, that often accompanies seafood recipes. Linguine looks like spaghetti, except it is slightly flattened. Literally means "little tongues."

Lumache. The name means "snails," which aptly describes this hooked pasta. It comes in several sizes.

Mezzani. A long, tubular pasta resembling a soda straw, or a thicker version of bucatini. The name may refer to a "go-between," which would reflect the ability of the sauce to literally "go-between" the pasta. Mezzani should not be confused with the pastas that begin with "*mezzi di . . . ,*" which means half-size.

Occhi. The name means "eyes," and it usually refers to a tiny, bead-like pasta with a dot or hole in the center. You will typically find it referred to as *occhi di lupo* (wolf eyes), or eyes of other animals such as a partridge, or elephant.

Orecchietti. Another pasta inspired by the human anatomy. Oval-shaped and slightly concave, this pasta is aptly named "ears."

Pappardelle. A wide, ribbon-like pasta that resembles lasagna. Literally translated, it means "long speech" or "long mouthful."

Penne. A short, tubular pasta cut diagonally on both ends. Penne comes in several dozen sizes, ranging from *penne grandi rigati* (large penne with ridges) to *pennette* (little penne). Penne means "plume" in Italian and refers to the old-fashioned writing instrument, the forerunner of the pen.

Perciatelli. A cousin of bucatini, this pasta is long and tubular, and resembles a soda straw. It is slightly thicker than bucatini. The name comes from the word *perciare* which means to make a hole.

Rigatoni. Another tubular pasta, known as the "pipe" (as in the pipe of a church organ). Rigatoni is usually ridged, about two inches long, and it can stand up to the heaviest sauce.

Ruote di Carro. True to its name, "cart wheels," this pasta is round, about the diameter of a nickel, and has spokes. A hearty pasta preferred in Southern Italy, ruote di carro is sometimes referred to as *rotelle*.

Sedani. The name literally means "celery." The pasta is tubular, about the thickness of a celery stalk, and measures about one and one-half inches in length. Usually smooth, some styles have ridges.

Spaghetti. Perhaps the most famous of all pastas, at least in America. A long and thin pasta, the origin of its name is somewhat vague, but it may be related to the word *spago*, which means "string." *Spaghettini* is a thinner version of spaghetti.

Stivaletti. A specialty pasta that I like to think was invented to celebrate the unification of Italy. "Stivaletti" means little boots, and the pasta does indeed have a fitting name.

Strangolopreti. Imagination runs wild when this title is translated; it means "that which strangles priests." A round, clumpy pasta somewhat like conchiglie, only narrower. One of the more plausible (if that word can be applied with a straight face) explanations for the name is that it refers to

---

HOW TO MAKE PASTA

The basic ingredients of homemade pasta, or pasta all'uova, are flour and eggs. Store-bought pasta, or pasta asciutta, is usually made with flour and water. You will need at least one whole egg for every cup of flour when working by hand. (These proportions may vary depending on the size of the eggs, the humidity, and the altitude.) If you use a pasta machine, you can make firmer pasta by adding fewer eggs. In either case, your eggs should be at room temperature. One egg and one-cup of flour will make about one-half pound of fresh pasta. The ingredients can be doubled or tripled and still handled effectively. If you need more pasta, though, you would be better off to use a pasta machine, which will save time and energy.

Step One: Pour flour onto a smooth wooden or formica table, and make a mound. Form a crater in the center of the mound; crack open the eggs, and pour them into the crater.

Step Two: Mix the eggs with a fork, gathering and blending the flour gradually into the center. Continue until the flour becomes doughy and can be worked by hand.

Step Three: Knead the dough by folding it, and then flattening and stretching it against the table with the palms of your hands. Knead the dough until it becomes smooth and elastic, and has a consistent texture without dry lumps or holes. Then place the dough under a bowl.

Step Four: After 20 minutes, cut the dough in half (or in quarters, etc., depending on volume), and roll out one-half at a time. Your hands, table, and rolling pin should be coated with flour to prevent sticking. Flatten the dough into a broad circle. Start in the center, and expand the circle of dough by rolling the pin away from you. Turn the sheet of dough periodically. Press the dough as thin as possible without breaking it; add flour as needed to keep the pin from sticking.

Step Five: Let the dough dry for about 10 minutes. Then cut it with a pasta die; or, roll it up and cut narrow strips (width-wise) with a knife. Unwind the strips, and you have homemade fettuccine, ready to be cooked!

A variety of tools, machines, and utensils are available for making pasta, from the electric-powered models that do everything from mixing and kneading the dough to producing the desired shape, to the lowly but functional rolling pin.

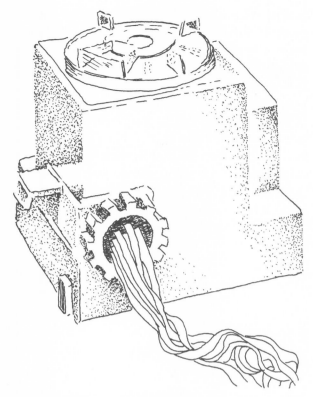

Vermicelli. A long, thin pasta, slightly thinner than spaghetti, and well-known in America. The name for this pasta shows that Italians spare no description for the sake of delicacy, because vermicelli literally means "worms."

Ziti. A broad, tubular pasta, often served with tomato sauces at weddings. Ziti is derived from the word *zita*, which means "bride" in Neopolitan dialect. (I have never been to an Italian wedding that did not serve ziti!) The pasta comes in several sizes, from long *(ziti lunghi)* to short *(ziti corti).* Some styles are smooth and others have ridges.

Any one of these pastas can be purchased at a well-stocked Italian grocery store. In fact, I urge you to try different shapes, because, despite the similarities in ingredients, the various shapes have different culinary virtues. Of course, you can also make any one of these pastas by hand (or with a pasta machine), provided you have the proper dies and enough patience. I must confess, however, that I have never had the compunction to make the more elaborate styles, such as bucatini or ruote di carro. But don't let that dissuade you if you prefer homemade pasta.

the gluttony of clergymen. Not too absurd when you consider that the Church, particularly in Italy, was very wealthy during the Renaissance and Baroque eras, while the majority of people were poor and starving.

Tagliatelle. A long, ribbon-like pasta, strikingly similar to fettuccine. Tagliatelle, often made with eggs and flour, is said to have been inspired by the golden locks of Lucrezia Borgia.

Tagliolini. A wispy egg pasta, slightly thinner than tagliatelle. Brittle when dry, it is wrapped for storing and looks like a nest.

Tortellini. A short, ribbon-like pasta characterized by it twisted shape and meat filling. Tortellini means "little twists."

Trenette. A thinner version of linguine, although it does retain the slightly flattened contour of linguine. Trenette originated in Genoa, but today it is more commonly found around Naples. It is frequently used in seafood dishes.

Tufoli. Similar to its more familiar cousin *rigatoni*, tufoli is a stubby tube with smooth sides. About two inches long, the pasta is usually served with thick meaty tomato sauces.

Uova di Pesce. Perhaps the simplest design of any pasta. Used mostly for pasta *in brodo* (in soups), uova di pesce, which means fish eggs, are tiny beads of pasta, about the size of caviar.

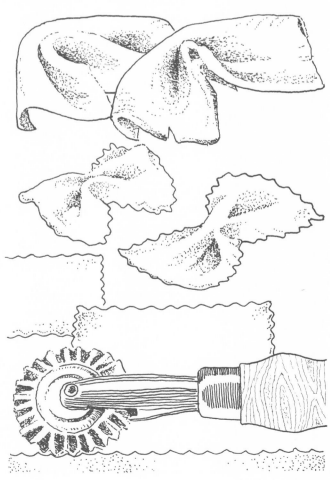

Whether you make your own pasta or buy it at a grocery store, you should know the difference between high quality and low quality pasta, and how to recognize each. Although all pasta is made from wheat flour, some flours are made from hard grain wheat, and others are made from soft grain wheat. *Hard grain flour makes a superior pasta.* In Italy, after centuries of debate (involving several Papal decrees on the making of pasta), the government began to regulate the making of pasta. Today, all pasta manufacturers in Italy (over 400 of them) must use hard grains, which are known as *grano duro*, or "durum wheat."

The white flour that Americans are most familiar with is made from soft grain wheat. In Italy, soft grain is called *grano tenero*, and it produces a flour known as farina. Soft grain is lighter than hard grain, both in color and in weight. The core of the soft grain is pure white. When ground it produces a powdery flour that is excellent for breads and pastries. Hard grain is nearly double the size of soft grain; it has an amber color and a slightly elongated shape. When ground, hard grain produces a coarse flour (known as *semola*) that resembles fine yellow sand. When the two flours are compared, the difference is striking.

With either grain; flour is made from the core of the kernel; the core accounts for about eighty percent of the grain. Known as the endosperm, the core is encased by several distinct layers. The outermost layer is called the wheat germ; it is responsible for reproduction. The second three layers make up the bran, and the fifth and sixth layers are considered by-products, which are used for animal feed. (Whole wheat flour is made by grinding the whole kernel, before any layers are removed. That accounts for the uneven color.)

If you have ever made glue by mixing flour and water over a low flame, then you know that wheat flour has a special property: starch. Starch is sticky; when a pasta releases too much starch, it usually sticks together when cooked, and you end up with a gooey mess. Ordinarily, however, starch in pasta poses no problem if the pasta contains enough gluten. That is, all wheat flours, whether from hard or soft grain, contain starch, but hard grain contains a stronger, more flexible gluten. Gluten is the substance that holds the starch together; it is elastic and tough. Gluten can be described as a net that holds the starch: the more tightly woven the net, the better the gluten, and the better quality pasta.

Because pasta made from soft grain has weaker gluten, it tends to be mushy and sticky when cooked. Poor quality brands will even turn the cooking water milky, because of the high amount of starch being released. Pasta made from hard grain will remain firm when cooked; it will not stick together even after it has been drained, and it will be flexible. Once you eat a hard grain pasta, I guarantee you will not go back to eating soft grain pasta—the hard grain is that superior!

Hard grain pasta takes slightly longer to cook (about fifteen minutes) than soft grain pasta, but it cooks more evenly. When cooked, soft grain pasta often has an inconsistent texture: the inside is firmer than the outside. Cooking pasta may be simple, but cooking pasta *correctly* can be tricky. There is no surer way to ruin a delicately seasoned sauce than to pour it over overcooked pasta. Another advantage of hard grain pasta is that it is more difficult to overcook. Even if it cooks a little too long, it usually retains a certain measure of firmness.

The real test for determining when a pasta is cooked properly is simply to bite into it. The pasta should have body and definition; it should be tender but firm. Italians refer to this quality with the inexact term *pasta al dente*, which literally means "pasta to the tooth." (Older cookbooks often recommended that the way to tell if pasta, particularly long, thin pasta, was cooked was to throw a strand at a wall. If the pasta stuck, it was finished. Well, nothing could be further from the truth, because if you use a high quality durum wheat pasta, the pasta will *never* stick.)

The problem with making homemade pasta from hard grain flour is that, if you make it by hand, it becomes difficult to knead and roll. The same toughness that enables it to hold the starch will resist your attempts to stretch it out. Making egg pasta will help, and sometimes adding a tablespoon of olive oil per pound of dough will also make the hard grain dough more pliable. Fortunately, as the interest in pasta and cereal grains increases in the United States, more and more retailers are stocking varieties of flour, and you should have little trouble finding a flour that you can work with.

One way around the difficulty of kneading hard grain dough by hand is to get a mechanical or electric pasta maker. The mechanical models still require muscle power, but they can reduce the amount of exertion required. The electric models can save you a lot of trouble, and they usually come with a variety of dies for making different pasta shapes. I recommend, however, that you follow the instructions for making pasta that come with most electric models. If all attempts at making homemade pasta from hard grain fail, then you can always take solace in knowing that the commercial pastas made from hard grain are excellent and widely available.

In summary, the design and ingredients of pasta should not be taken for granted. When a recipe calls for a specific pasta shape, you should do your best to find it. Using hard grain pasta in recipes is perhaps the most telling difference between pasta dishes made in America (even in expensive restaurants) and pasta dishes made in Italy. A high quality pasta is as important as the ingredients of your sauce.

Pasta made from durum wheat flour will not turn the cooking water milky, and it will not stick together when cooked. Durum wheat pasta, when cooked, has a smooth, nervy, and flexible quality, and it always stays firm. The history of pasta, as we know it, may be part fact and part fiction, but I do know that if you follow the simple rules for making and cooking pasta (and for buying it), your recipes will be more authentic and superior. All this proves, with all due respect to Marco Polo, that you do not have to travel far to discover the delight of a well-made dish of pasta.

CHOOSING THE BEST
SEASONINGS
AND
INGREDIENTS

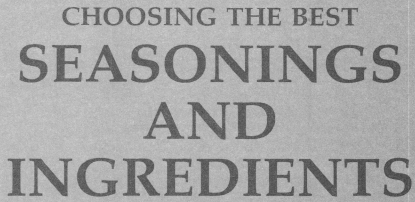

Choosing the

When it comes to cooking, Italians have a saying: *"Quello che ci metti, ci ritrovi,"* which means "What you put in, you will find."

I cannot think of a better phrase to emphasize the importance of choosing the best seasonings and ingredients for your recipes. The more care you take in selecting and preparing your ingredients, the more successful you will be in eliciting their distinctive flavors. Quality should never be compromised, even if the recipe calls for only small quantities of seasonings. A pinch of marjoram, a dash of hot pepper, a dusting of Romano can be the difference between a good recipe and a superb recipe.

Italian cuisine is the mother cuisine of French cooking. But unlike French sauces, which are blends of spices and flavors, Italian sauces have a special clarity and definition. Every ingredient speaks for itself, and the way individual flavors play off one another is the true art of Italian cooking.

In fact, you can take this insistence on quality one step further, as Italians do, and adopt the "marketing" approach to cooking pasta recipes. When planning your meal, don't choose your recipe first; start by visiting the market and seeing what looks best. If you choose a recipe, and then have to settle for dry basil, or for tomatoes that are not quite ripe, or for bitter-tasting eggplant, your recipe will be cheated.

There are two types of seasonings. *Herbs,* such as basil and parsley, are small plants that die at the end of the growing season. They are characterized by their lack of woody branches. *Spices,* such as nutmeg and saffron, are aromatic plants, sometimes trees, that produce pods, berries, or bark that can be dried and ground.

Always try to use fresh herbs (most of which can be grown at home), although in some cases dried herbs can be used. Fresh herbs make the task of cooking much easier. They add spark and zest to the most common recipes, and they are the mark of authentic Italian cooking. Spices are almost always dried before they can be used. But you should try to buy them whole and grind them yourself, because spices release the most flavor when they are first ground.

Basil. Sweet basil is an aromatic herb with glossy leaves that can grow to an inch or more. Basil is in the mint family, and the plant bears some resemblance to peppermint. Basil should always be used fresh, never dried. Widely used throughout Italy, basil is the mark of cooking in Liguria, where pesto originated.

Marjoram. Sweet marjoram is a small bushy plant with velvety leaves and pink flowering tops. A relative of oregano, marjoram is milder and sweeter, but is used in the same way as oregano.

Oregano. The oregano imported from Europe is actually wild marjoram, although much of the oregano in the United States comes from Mexico. A sturdy perennial with purple, white, or pink flowers, oregano is characteristic of Southern Italian cooking. Because durable oregano holds its flavor well, it can be used when dried.

Parsley. A popular herb commonly grown at home. Flat-leafed Italian parsley is preferred over the curly variety, because it has more flavor. As far as I can tell, dried parsley has no taste.

Rosemary. An evergreen herb that can grow to several feet. Because this pungent herb retains its flavor well, it can be used dried, though fresh is preferred. When using small amounts for seasoning, crush or crumble the leaves to bring out the most flavor.

Sage Leaves. A small shrub, with wide leaves and blue, purple, pink, or white flowers, sage is native to southern Europe. Its leaves make a delightful seasoning, and should be used fresh. Dried whole leaves are acceptable, but never use crushed, dried leaves.

Tarragon. A perennial shrub that grows up to two feet high, tarragon is also native to southern Europe. It has a distinctive anise or licorice flavor that goes well in cream sauces.

Thyme. A very small plant, no more than eight inches high with tiny leaves. Thyme, a native of Italy, has a bittersweet taste and penetrating fragrance. It compliments seafood recipes. Most stores sell this plant dried.

Black Pepper. Perhaps the most popular and familiar of all. It originated along the Malabar Coast of India. The berries of this vine-like plant are green, but ripen to red and then black. When ripe, they are picked and dried, and become familiar as peppercorns.

White Pepper. A milder form of black pepper. When ripe, the black hull of the pepper berry is removed, exposing the white inside. Then the berry is dried and ground.

Cayenne Pepper. This spice is made by grinding the pod and seed of the capsicum plant—more commonly known as the chili pepper. If you are a fan of chili, then you know how hot this seasoning can be. It originated in the Cayenne district of Africa.

Curry. A wonderfully pervasive spice that originated in India, where curry is used in many dishes.

BESCIAMELLA SAUCE

Besciamella sauce can be used as a flavoring or as a base for pasta sauces. A creamy, white sauce that originated in Florence, besciamella was first brought to France by Catherine de' Medici, who married the heir to the French throne in 1533. Today, French cooks call this sauce bechamel.

In Italy, besciamella is served over cooked vegetables, or it is combined with specific tomato sauces to make them creamier and more palatable. Besciamella, despite its royal associations, can be made from the most basic ingredients in minutes. You will need the following ingredients.

    1¼ cups of warm milk
    3 tbsp. of butter
    4 tsp. of flour
    salt and pepper

Melt butter in small sauce pan or double boiler. Slowly mix in flour until a paste forms. Over low heat, add warm milk, stirring slowly until the sauce becomes creamy. Salt and pepper to taste. Makes about one cup.

It has a strong peppery flavor and a light yellow color. Commercial curry is actually a combination of various spices.

Nutmeg. A sweet and mild spice with a nutty flavor. Nutmeg originated in North Africa and was first brought to the West Indies. It grows in a large pod, somewhat like a chestnut, on the nutmeg tree. The husk of the pod is removed, and the seed is ground to produce a powder.

Peperoncino. Italians like to dry vegetables, particularly peppers, by sewing them together and hanging them from a wall or doorway. For peppers, drying brings out their hotness. Peperoncino is made by drying long hot peppers. They are usually green or yellow, but turn increasingly red as they mature. When thoroughly dried, they become brittle. The pepper is then crushed, seeds and all, and sprinkled into sauces or on soups for a heady, mouth-watering flavoring.

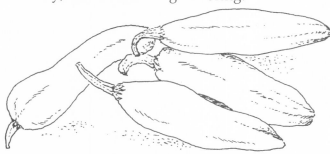

Saffron. An aromatic and bitter spice made from the pistil of the saffron crocus, which grows wild and is cultivated in North Africa. Saffron usually comes in powdered form, with a dark red color. Use it sparingly; not only is saffron expensive, it is also pervasive. A pinch will turn a full pot of cream sauce bright yellow.

Butter. Almost any brand of butter will suffice, provided it is "unsalted."

Garlic. The notion that Italian recipes call for copious amounts of garlic is false. When properly used in sauces, garlic flavorings should be subtle and enhancing, not overbearing. Look for fresh garlic with plump cloves.

Capers. Capers are flower buds of the caperbush, which grows wild and is cultivated in Italy. The buds are tiny, but they have a sharp, penetrating flavor. They can be bought in many stores and typically come packed in salt or vinegar.

Olive Oil. Extra virgin olive oil, which is made from the first pressing of olives, is preferred. The best olive oil should be light green and have the delicate fragrance and taste of fresh olives. You do not have to buy Italian olive oil only; Spain, France, Greece, and California produce first-rate olive oils.

Red Wine Vinegar. As the name suggests, this vinegar is made from fermented red wine. High quality red wine vinegar is palatable, not acidy. It should be purchased plain, without added seasonings.

Prosciutto. Italian prosciutto is unsmoked, salt-cured ham. It is cured for at least nine months. The best prosciutto comes from Parma, where the farmers' know-how and the region's climate is said to produce the best ham. Although real Italian prosciutto is unavailable in America (it can carry a virus that is harmless to humans but dangerous to American swine), some American prosciuttos are excellent. In recipes, you can substitute with cooked, unsmoked ham.

Pancetta. An Italian bacon, salt-cured, either smoked or unsmoked. It is difficult to find in America, but you can substitute with smoked bacon that has been blanched in boiling water (for three minutes) to remove the smoked flavor.

Mortadella. A delicately flavored baloney that is a specialty of Bologna (where the name "bologna" or "baloney" originated). The meat is made by combining ground pork and veal with pieces of white pork fat, pepper grains, pistachio nuts, and other seasonings. Mortadella used to be made (around 1400) by crushing pork with a large mortar and pestle. The specially designed mortar was called *"un mortaio della carne di maiale,"* which means "mortar for the meat of a pig." Over time, the name was shortened to mortadella.

Pinoli Nuts. These tiny, delicate nuts are known as pine nuts in America. They grow wild in Italy. Pinoli nuts are sweet and chewy, and they are used in pastries (especially to make holiday cookies) and in recipes such as pesto.

Tomatoes. Although there are dozens of types of tomatoes, Italians prefer the plum tomato for sauces. Interestingly enough, the tomato, which is often associated with Italian cooking, was first introduced in Italy in the 1500s. The tomato, which at that time was small and yellow, was brought to Europe from Mexico by Cortez. The Italians adopted it and called it *pomo d'oro,* which means golden apple. Cultivated for centuries, the plum tomato (pomodoro) has become red.

Whenever preparing a recipe with tomatoes, you will find it worthwhile to use fresh pomodoro tomatoes. They are easy to prepare; simply boil them for two minutes. The skins can then be readily removed.

Canned tomatoes may also be used; however, make sure that they are plum tomatoes. The best plum tomatoes come from the San Marzano area, near Naples. If you use imported brands, look for "San Marzano" on the label. Most canned tomatoes contain pulp and juice. When a recipe indicates one-cup of tomatoes, use two-fifths juice and three-fifths pulp. This ratio will balance the flavor, and keep the sauce from becoming too dry.

HOMEMADE BROTH

A few pasta sauces call for broth. Although canned broth, or broth made from bouillon, can be used, I prefer homemade, because it adds far more flavor. Fortunately, homemade broth can be stored effectively, and used when needed. Meat broth should be made from chicken or beef, or from a combination of the two. Meats such as lamb or pork are not recommended, because their distinct flavors tend to dominate pasta sauces. A delightful broth can be made from the following ingredients.

    2 lbs. of beef, with soup bone
    1½ lbs. of chicken pieces
    1 medium-sized onion, peeled, cut in half
    1 carrot, peeled, cut up
    1 celery stalk, cut up
    6 sprigs fresh parsley
    3 ripe plum tomatoes, cut in half
    1 tsp. salt

Place ingredients in a large pot, and add enough water to cover them by two inches. Cover the pot and bring the mixture to a boil. Reduce heat and simmer for two hours, until the water reduces and the broth reaches desired flavor and consistency. Pour broth through a strainer into a large bowl, cover, and refrigerate. Fats that congeal on the surface can be easily removed. Place broth in small plastic containers, and freeze for future use.

Cheeses

In Italy, cheese-making is an admired art and an important industry. About one-half of the milk produced in Italy goes into making more than 350 different cheeses. Italians have made cheese for centuries; Parmesan was first produced for mass consumption over 1,000 years ago. In ancient times, cheese was valued so highly in Italy that it was considered more reliable than currency, and it was used for money. Whether used as a seasoning, stuffing, table cheese, or dessert, cheese is a fundamental part of Italian cooking.

Parmigiano Reggiano. In America, we know this cheese as Parmesan. It is a popular cheese used primarily for grating. Produced in northern Italy only from April 15 through November 11, Parmesan is made to strict specifications. It should be purchased in chunks, and grated just before using.

Pecorino Romano. This cheese is familiar to Americans as Romano. It is sharp, pungent, and slightly salty. Used primarily for grating, a good Romano feels oily. It is made from sheep's milk that has been curdled with rennet, which is a coagulating agent made from the inner stomach lining of an unweaned lamb. Buy this cheese in chunks and grate only before using.

Ricotta. A light, fluffy, moist cheese, not unlike cottage cheese. Ricotta is used as a stuffing for *pasta ripieni*, and also in desserts.

Mozzarella. A mellow cheese that was originally made from the milk of a water buffalo. Today, Italians also use cow's milk to make mozzarella. American versions are made only from cow's milk. When heated, mozzarella can be stretched to unimaginable lengths. Italian mozzarella, which comes packed in a milky liquor, is softer than its American counterpart, so if you use domestic brands, let it sit out and soften before use.

Fontina. A sweet, delicately flavored cheese made in Northern Italy, in the Val d'Aosta region. Named after Mount Font, fontina is used widely in dishes calling for melted cheese.

Gorgonzola. A tangy and crumbly cheese made from cow's milk. It resembles blue cheese. Gorgonzola originated from a town northeast of Milan; the town is called (what else?) Gorgonzola.

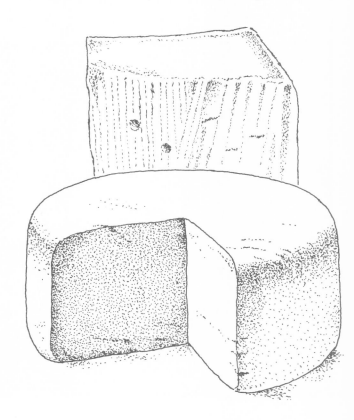

ITALIAN COOKWARE

Italian

The kitchen utensils for preparing pasta and sauces are familiar to most Americans. The average kitchen is already equipped with the two essentials: a broad skillet, and a pot for boiling pasta. Of course, an assortment of knives, spoons, pots, pans, and other utensils can also come in handy, and a few specialty items, like the garlic press or the mortar and pestle, may be the only acceptable way to prepare garlic and basil. Nowadays, so many gadgets and tools are available that "well-equipped" kitchens can rival the supply depot at an Army base. And frankly, I am often overwhelmed by the variety of cookware stocked by the typical cooking store. Although pasta-making equipment can be expensive, you do not need to spend money to make pasta or to prepare expert recipes. Nonetheless, some cookware deserves mention here, because it can facilitate the joy of cooking Italian-style.

Large Pot. A sturdy, heat-conductive pot (with two handles) for boiling water is essential. The pot should be able to hold six to eight quarts of water easily, along with two pounds of pasta.

Colander. A metal or plastic colander should be large enough to easily accommodate two-pounds of pasta. It should have plenty of large holes, and be able to stand on its own in the sink. The colander should not be confused with the strainer.

Skillets. At least three skillets, in different sizes, can be used for sauces. They should be sturdy, with straight sides and flat bottoms, and have heat-resistant handles. Non-stick skillets are recommended for several recipes.

Cheese Grater. There are several types of cheese graters. I use a hand-held file grater for large chunks of cheese, and a washboard-type grater

Cookware

for smaller pieces. The washboard grater is truly a fascinating device, with several types of grating surfaces, it can cut almost any type of cheese in several different ways. For grating large amounts of cheese, you can even get a hand-cranked machine that mounts onto a kitchen table.

Double Boiler. Italians call this a *bagnomaria*, which is a pot within a pot. The bottom pot boils water, and the top pot holds the sauce so that it cooks slowly and evenly. The double boiler is excellent for cooking delicate sauces.

Mortar and Pestle. An ancient device with two parts. The mortar is a heavy cup, usually made from wood or marble, that functions as a crushing surface. The pestle, also made of wood or marble, is a thick rod used to crush herbs and spices placed in the mortar. They may be familiar to you as a pharmacist's cup. They have been used traditionally to crush basil and make pesto.

Both pestle and pesto come from the Italian word *pestare*, which means to crush.

Strainer. The best strainers are made of thin but sturdy wire mesh, with tiny holes. Either the self-standing model or the model that fits into a pot are acceptable. A broad, flat-bottomed strainer can also be used effectively to remove seeds and pulp from tomatoes. Place the tomatoes in the strainer and then force them through the mesh with a spoon.

Vegetable Grinder. A pot with a wire mesh bottom and a curved rotating blade used to grind and strain vegetables such as tomatoes. The blade is cranked by hand. The grinder has the same effect on tomatoes as the strainer (described above), only it makes the task easier.

Two-fisted Chopper. The best tool for chopping and mincing large quantities of herbs and vegetables. The chopper is really a knife shaped like a half-moon with two knobs, one at either end. You simply hold onto the knobs and rock the device back and forth on a cutting board.

Garlic Press. A small, hand-held tool that works on the same principle as a nutcracker. The garlic press has a small chamber, about the size of a garlic clove. Place a clove in the chamber, bring the two handles together and squeeze. The garlic will be crushed and, thereby, it will release the most flavor.

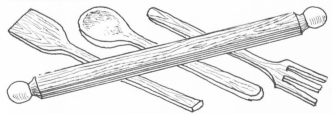

Matterello. An Italian version of the rolling pin, used for flattening pasta dough. The matterello is about 24 inches long, and thinner in diameter than a standard rolling pin. Moreover, it has no handles, so you roll it like a pipe.

Wooden Spoons and Forks. Wooden utensils for stirring pasta while it cooks, or for mixing sauces, are preferred. They do not interfere with the taste of the sauce, as metal utensils do, and they are blunt and porous, which make them well-suited for stirring cooked pasta. A well-seasoned wooden cooking spoon is the mark of the experienced Italian cook.

Serving Platters. Serving platters and bowls should be large enough to contain the pasta and sauce easily, and should always be warmed in advance.

Pasta Makers. A wide range of pasta-making machines are now on the market. They range from inexpensive models that are hand-cranked to expensive electric models that soon may be classified as robots. (They do everything from mixing and kneading the pasta dough, to producing fancy pasta designs. Well worth the investment.) However, each pasta machine has a set of instructions for making pasta, and you should follow them closely.

Bigolaro. An interesting apparatus for history buffs, though I am told some people in Italy still use them. The bigolaro may be the first pasta machine ever invented; it was used in the Middle Ages to make *bigoli*, an early form of pasta. It looks like a cross between a wooden bench and a vegetable grinder. The cook would straddle the bench and operate a hand-crank that would force dough through a tube. The bigoli noodles would come out the other end.

Chitarra. Another old pasta-maker, so named because it resembles a guitar, or lute. The chitarra is made by stretching metal wires across a wooden frame. The wires are closely spaced. A sheet of rolled pasta dough is placed across the wires and then pressed with a small roller. The wires effectively slice the dough into thin strips, resembling spaghetti. This device is still commonly used throughout Italy.

Slotted Spoon. At least one large, slotted spoon will be needed to retrieve garlic cloves and sprigs of herbs from sauces. Either wood or metal will do.

Clam Knife. A dull, flat knife with a wide blade, perfect for opening fresh oysters and clams. The knife gives adequate leverage and guards against nasty nicks and cuts. However, sometimes oysters and clams are just too difficult to open. In that case, place them in the sink, fill the sink with an inch or two of hot tap water, wait two minutes, and they will open on their own.

Olive Pitter. Unless you have an olive tree in your backyard, and plenty of fresh olives to be pitted, this device can be classified as a luxury item. Yet, it is the only effective way I know for pitting an olive without destroying the olive in the process. The olive pitter is a hand-held instrument, somewhat like the garlic crusher. You place an olive in a small open-ended chamber and squeeze the pitter's handles. A pin is driven straight through the olive, and the pit is ejected.

Certainly no kitchen is complete without a full compliment of kitchen knives, sauce pans, and other basics like a sturdy cutting board. But it is easy to lose sight, in our technological era, of the fact that many Italian pasta recipes were originally rustic dishes. Some were made by shepherds, others invented by sailors and teamsters, who did not have the convenience of a roof, let alone a kitchen. In keeping with the authentic spirit of these pasta recipes, use your imagination and be resourceful, not only in inventing recipes, but also in preparing the ingredients.

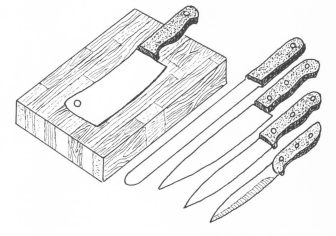

RECIPES

Fettuccine all'Alfredo

Fettuccine Alfredo

1 pound egg fettuccine
1 cup of unsalted butter

2 cups of Parmesan, grated
1/4 cup cooking water

Place serving platter in hot water until the platter becomes very hot; remove the platter and dry it.
Cut butter into small pieces and place them on the platter. The butter, in contact with the platter, should start to melt.
Meanwhile, cook fettuccine in slightly salted water, and drain. (Be sure to save some of the water.)
Place fettuccine neatly on top of the butter and pour the water evenly over it.
Completely cover the fettuccine, so that it cannot be seen, with an even layer of grated Parmesan.
Bring the platter to the table, mix with a flourish in front of your guests, and serve immediately.
(Obviously, this recipe must be timed perfectly, so that the platter will be hot enough to melt the butter and cheese.)

WINES: Frascati superiore, Pinot grigio, Verdicchio, Orvieto bianco

PASTA: Egg fettuccine *only*

All the recipes contained in this book call for one-pound of pasta. The proportions, however, may be increased or decreased as necessary. If a pasta recipe is served as a first course, one-pound will satisfy four to six adults. If it is served as a main course, one-pound will satisfy two to four adults. One-third of a pound per person is an average pasta serving. One-half pound will satisfy even the most voracious pasta lover.

This recipe was given to me by Alfredo Di Lelio, who is the grandson of the original Alfredo and the proprietor of "l'Originale Alfredo all'Augusteo," the legendary restaurant in Rome.

Alfredo warns, however, that making this authentic and famous recipe can be difficult to duplicate even though the ingredients are quite simple, because his family has always had its ingredients specially made. They make their own fettuccine from the best semola flour, made from hard durum wheat, and fresh eggs. The butter is particularly rich and creamy (This often leads people to believe that cream is added). And the Parmesan, also specially made for the Di Lelio's, should be cut from the core of the cheese block. The Parmesan should be young—no older than 14 months.

Whenever in Rome, you should make a visit to "Augusteo" and have Alfredo serve up his specialty. The artistry and flair with which he mixes the fettuccine is truly inspiring. When his guests are of world-renowned fame (and his restaurant is covered with photographs of world leaders and legendary figures), he mixes the fettuccine with a solid gold fork and spoon, which were given to his grandfather Alfredo in 1927 by Mary Pickford and Douglas Fairbanks in recognition of his masterful serving technique. (The golden utensils originally weighed one and one-half pounds, but over the years they have lost nearly two ounces through wear and tear.)

A determined cook can come close to matching the quality of Alfredo's ingredients by making the fettuccine and butter, and purchasing the best imported Parmesan.

Make the fettuccine, as described in Chapter II, from semola flour, made only from hard durum wheat, and the freshest eggs. This may be difficult to do by hand, so you may need to use a mechanical pasta maker. Creamier butter than the store-bought kind can also be made simply; whip heavy cream until it turns to butter. Moreover, try to purchase imported Parmesan that has not been aged longer than 14 months. Young Parmesan has a pale color and soft consistency—and all blocks of Parmesan are stamped on the side with their date of manufacture. Have the cheese shop cut you a chunk from the center core of the block. This may raise a few eyebrows when you tell them that you intend to grate it, because the center is expensive and a highly regarded table cheese. But just tell them you are following the specific instructions of a master chef—Alfredo Di Lelio.

Tagliatelle con prosciutto e panna

Tagliatelle with prosciutto and cream

1 pound tagliatelle
2/3 cup heavy cream
1/3 cup prosciutto, minced
1/2 cup Parmesan cheese, grated

6 tablespoons butter
1 tablespoon parsley, chopped
1/8 teaspoon white pepper

Boil tagliatelle in salted water.
Meanwhile, melt butter over very low heat in a large non-stick skillet.
Drain cooked tagliatelle and place in skillet with melted butter.
At low heat, toss continuously with 2 wooden spoons while adding cream, prosciutto, and pepper until all ingredients are blended.
Top servings with chopped parsley and grated Parmesan.

WINES: Rosé, Chiaretto

ALTERNATE PASTA: Fettuccine

Adding cream to pasta sauces creates a smoother, more delicate texture.
In Italy, cooks use fresh cream or a type of evaporated cream that does not require refrigeration.
The Emilia-Romagna region, where Besciamella originated in the 1500s, boasts the most cream recipes.

Tagliatelle alla bolognese

Tagliatelle Bologna

1 pound egg-tagliatelle
1 cup tomatoes, peeled, cut in pieces
1 cup dry red wine
1 cup beef broth
2 strips bacon, finely chopped
1/2 pound ground beef (or combination of
   beef, pork, veal)
6 tablespoons butter
1/2 tablespoon parsley, finely chopped

pinch nutmeg
1 clove garlic, finely chopped
1 medium-sized onion, finely chopped
1 carrot, finely chopped
1 celery stalk, finely chopped
5 tablespoons Parmesan cheese, grated
salt and pepper

Place 3 tablespoons butter and bacon in a large skillet and melt butter over low heat.
Add garlic, onion, carrot and celery (which can be chopped together in a blender) and sauté for about ten minutes.
Stir continuously. Add ground meat and break up with a fork.
When meat has browned, add salt and pepper, parsley and a pinch of nutmeg.
Pour in wine and simmer until all the wine has evaporated.
Mix in tomatoes, add broth, cover and simmer over medium heat for at least one hour.
Stir occasionally. If sauce becomes too thick before the hour, add more broth.
At the end of the hour sauce should be thick.
Place cooked pasta in a serving dish with a few tablespoons of butter.
Mix in half of the sauce. The remaining sauce can be placed over individual servings.
Top with grated Parmesan.

WINES: Chianti classico, Barolo, Gattinara

ALTERNATE PASTA: egg-Tagliolini, egg-Fettuccine, Fettuccine, Tagliatelle

*As the name suggests, this recipe originated in Bologna, the capital of Emilia-Romagna.
Ravioli, tortellini, and agnolotti all come from this region as well as parmigiano-reggiano (Parmesan),
one of the most famous cheeses in the world, and prosciutto di Parma, the reknowned salt-cured ham.
It is little wonder that Emilia-Romagna has become synonymous with fine dining.*

Spaghetti alla carbonara

Coalminer's Spaghetti

1 pound spaghetti	2 tablespoons olive oil
7 strips of lean bacon, chopped	4 tablespoons butter
1/2 cup of light cream	1/3 cup Romano cheese, grated
3 eggs	salt and freshly ground pepper

All ingredients should be at room temperature before starting.
In a skillet large enough to accommodate cooked pasta, sauté bacon in oil and butter.
In a bowl beat eggs; add cheese, a dash of salt and mix.
Pour in cream and mix. While preparing sauce, cook pasta al dente, drain and place in skillet with bacon over a low heat.
Mix thoroughly. Remove from heat and add in egg mixture.
Mix rapidly until eggs coagulate. Top with freshly ground black pepper and serve immediately.

WINES: Bardolino, Merlot, Corvo rosso, Chianti classico

ALTERNATE PASTA: Bucatini, Vermicelli

Carbonara, which means "of the coalminer," was originally made with heaps of black pepper—hence the name. In many regions of Italy, one-third cup of dry white wine is added to the sauce immediately after the bacon has been sautéed. The sauce is then allowed to simmer until the wine evaporates.

Spaghetti chi vruoccoli arriminati

Spaghetti with cauliflower

1 pound spaghetti
1 pound cauliflower, boiled
1 cup tomatoes, peeled, cut in pieces
1 cup water
8 tablespoons olive oil
3 tablespoons raisins

3 tablespoons pinoli nuts
2 garlic cloves
5 tablespoons Parmesan cheese, grated
2 tablespoons parsley, finely chopped
salt and pepper

Place raisins in luke warm water for 20 minutes until they soften; strain, and dry on a paper towel.
Meanwhile, in a large skillet, sauté garlic until golden brown.
Cut up cooked cauliflower and add to skillet.
Simmer for 10 minutes and break up cauliflower into small pieces with a wooden spoon.
Remove garlic, pour in tomatoes and water.
Bring mixture to a rapid boil, and then lower heat and simmer for 10 minutes.
Salt and pepper to taste. Add softened raisins and continue simmering for 5 minutes.
Mix in pinoli nuts and parsley, and stir.
Cook and strain pasta, and then add pasta to the skillet, mixing thoroughly.
Remove from heat, cover, and let sit for 5 minutes.
Serve with grated Parmesan.

WINES: Cabernet, Valpolicella, Merlot

ALTERNATE PASTA: Vermicelli, Linguine, Trenette

This recipe originated in Sicily, where vegetables are often used in pasta sauces.
Pinoli nuts and raisins, although unusual in most recipes, are frequently used in Sicilian dishes; they tend to sweeten the sauce.
"Vruoccoli arriminati" means "broccoli turned over," or mixed up, so named because the cook must continuously mix the vegetable until it breaks up into little pieces.
Broccoli in Italy means any one of the vegetables in the broccoli family, but this recipe is most often made with cauliflower.

Trenette al pesto

Trenette with pesto sauce

1 pound trenette
1 cup fresh basil leaves, in small pieces
1/2 garlic clove, finely chopped
3 tablespoons pinoli nuts, crushed

3 tablespoons Romano cheese, grated
8 tablespoons olive oil
pinch salt

Combine all ingredients (placing oil in first), except pasta and cheese, in a blender and crush until mixture is blended and of a smooth consistency.
(Ingredients may also be crushed with a mortar and pestle, as originally done in Genoa.)
Remove ingredients from blender, place in a bowl and add cheese.
Mix well. Cook pasta al dente, strain, and place in warm serving dish.
Add in pesto sauce and mix well.
Or, serve pasta in separate dishes and top each individual portion with a tablespoon or two of pesto sauce.

WINES: Tocai, Pinot grigio, Bianco di Montecarlo, Bianco delle Cinque Terre

ALTERNATE PASTA: Linguine

Pesto originated in Genoa, in the region of Liguria, where cooking with fresh herbs, especially basil, is an ancient practice.
In the 1500s, Genoese sailors spent many months at sea ferrying aromatic, exotic spices.
After living with strong, foreign smells, they desired nothing more than the fragrant herbs and vegetables of their native land.
The noticeable lack of spices in Genoese cooking is further testimony to the habits of the ancient seafarers.

Pesto sauce can be preserved for several months.
Store the sauce in a jar that has been boiled and sterilized; cover the pesto with about ½ inch of olive oil, and refrigerate.

Bucatini all'amatriciana
Bucatini Amatrice

1 pound bucatini
5 thick strips bacon, diced
2 cups tomatoes, peeled
1/4 cup olive oil
1/8 teaspoon crushed red pepper

4 garlic cloves
3 tablespoons red wine vinegar
2/3 cup Romano cheese, grated
pinch black pepper

In a large skillet, sauté garlic and bacon.
Add tomatoes, and squash them with a wooden spoon.
Cook 5–10 minutes over medium heat. Season with black and red pepper, and add vinegar.
Simmer until vinegar evaporates.
Cook pasta al dente, strain, and mix with sauce in a large serving bowl.
Top with grated Romano cheese.

WINES: Merlot, Corvo rosso, Cirò rosso

ALTERNATE PASTA: Perciatelli

This recipe originated in the town of Amatrice, a quaint medieval town atop a mountain north of Rome. The cooks of Amatrice combined their excellent pancetta (bacon) with their fine pecorino (Romano) cheese, a handful of mature tomatoes, and a spray of vinegar to create Bucatini all'Amatriciana—a dish that has become popular throughout Italy.

Spaghetti alla puttanesca

Spaghetti harlot style

1 pound spaghetti
3½ cups tomatoes, peeled
2 cloves garlic
ripe pitted black olives (5 per person)
1/3 cup olive oil

3 anchovie fillets
2 tablespoons of capers
1 tablespoon fresh parsley, chopped
1/4 teaspoon crushed red pepper
dash black pepper, freshly ground

In a large skillet, sauté garlic in oil and remove when golden brown.
Add anchovie fillets, and mash them with wooden spoon so they blend in with oil.
Add tomatoes, and break them up into smaller pieces.
Mix in capers and olives, and season with black and red pepper. Mix thoroughly.
Allow sauce to simmer for at least 20 minutes.
Sauce should not be thick. Top with chopped fresh parsley.

WINES: Chianti classico, Merlot, Barolo

ALTERNATE PASTA: Linguine, Vermicelli

"Puttanesca" comes from the word "puttana," or prostitute. Its common use as the name for a pasta recipe points up a difference in language. In Italian, some words or expressions considered vulgar in other languages are readily accepted and used colloquially.
Spaghetti alla Puttanesca tries in every way to be appealing, bewitching, and inviting.

Paglia e Fieno

Straw and Hay

1 pound Paglia e Fieno
1½ cups mushrooms, cleaned and sliced
1/2 cup shelled fresh peas
1/2 cup cooked ham, chopped
1¼ cups heavy cream

8 tablespoons Parmesan cheese, grated
1/8 cup melted butter
2 pinches nutmeg
salt and white pepper

In a large skillet, sauté peas in butter for 3−4 minutes.
Add ham, stir a few minutes, and then add mushrooms.
After 5 minutes, add cream and continue cooking for 10 minutes over low heat.
Stir continuously. Season with salt, pepper, and nutmeg.
Pour over paglia e fieno cooked al dente. Top with grated Parmesan.

WINES: Merlot, Valpolicella, Chianti Gallo Nero

Paglia e Fieno is made with green spinach noodles and egg noodles which resemble, when combined, straw and green hay. It originated in the Emilia-Romagna region, but is now popular throughout Italy, and is usually used with various white sauces.

Spaghetti paesani

Spaghetti country style

1 pound spaghetti
1 small onion, sliced
3/4 cup fresh parsley, chopped
4 tablespoons olive oil
1 garlic clove, finely chopped

1 teaspoon oregano
2 heaping tablespoons of plain bread
   crumbs
1/8 teaspoon freshly ground pepper
salt

Combine parsley, garlic and onion in a medium skillet with 2 tablespoons of olive oil, and sauté until onions are golden.
Season with freshly ground black pepper.
Add 1 teaspoon oregano and stir lightly.
In a separate pan, brown bread crumbs in remaining 2 tablespoons of olive oil and a little salt.
Place cooked pasta in heated serving bowl with sauce.
Mix well. Top with bread crumbs.

WINES: Orvieto bianco, Pinot grigio, Frascati, Bianco di Custoza

ALTERNATE PASTA: Linguine, Trenette, Vermicelli

In ancient times, bread crumbs mixed with water and honey made the first cookies.
Although breadcrumbs are an ingredient in many pasta sauces, you will find that using fresh *breadcrumbs will make a significant difference.*
Grate a high-quality Italian bread and dry in the oven at a low temperature.
They will keep nicely for a while if you store them in a small cotton or canvas bag (to keep the crumbs aerated) in the refrigerator.

Fusilli alla menta

Fusilli with mint

1 pound fusilli	2 garlic cloves, halved
1/2 cup basil leaves, in pieces	5 tablespoons olive oil
1 teaspoon fresh mint leaves, finely chopped	salt and pepper
1 tablespoon parsley, finely chopped	

Combine basil, mint, and parsley with 2 tablespoons of olive oil in a blender.
Blend into paste. In a large skillet lightly brown garlic cloves in 3 tablespoons of olive oil.
Remove pan from heat and mix in herb paste.
Cook and strain pasta, mix thoroughly with sauce. Salt and pepper to taste.

 **WINES**: Frascati, Orvieto bianco, Verdicchio

 **ALTERNATE PASTA**: Penne rigate

Mint, like basil, has the fragrance of summer, and is a popular ingredient used in many Italian pasta dishes. This delicate herb has a persistent aroma and taste that delightfully permeates the pasta.

Linguine alle erbe

Linguine with herbs

1 pound linguine
1/3 cup olive oil
1/3 cup fresh basil, finely chopped
1/3 cup fresh parsley, finely chopped

1 teaspoon fresh marjoram, finely chopped
1/2 teaspoon fresh thyme, finely chopped
2 pinches salt

Begin cooking pasta. A few minutes before pasta is done, sauté garlic in oil until golden.
Remove garlic from skillet and add parsley, marjoram, thyme, salt and simmer for 2 minutes.
Place cooked and strained pasta in skillet with herbs.
Mix thoroughly and rapidly. Top with basil. Serve immediately.

WINES: Frascati, Orvieto bianco, Corvo bianco

ALTERNATE PASTA: Spaghetti, Trenette

Penne al sugo di noci

Penne with walnut sauce

1 pound penne	3 tablespoons butter
2/3 cup walnut meat	1/3 cup Parmesan cheese, grated
2 teaspoons pinoli nuts	1/3 cup light cream
1 garlic clove, finely chopped	salt and pepper

On a cookie sheet, lightly toast walnut meats in oven.
Combine with pinoli nuts and crush in a blender or with mortar and pestle.
In a small skillet, sauté nuts lightly in butter.
Pour mixture into serving bowl, stir in one-half the cheese plus the garlic and cream; salt and pepper to taste, and mix thoroughly.
Add in pasta cooked al dente, and the remaining cheese. Mix well.

WINES: Merlot, Corvo rosso, Chianti classico

**ALTERNATE PASTA**: All Penne

In Italy, nuts are referred to as "frutta secca," or dried fruits, and they are served along with fresh fruits in restaurants.
In pasta recipes, nuts are often used as a garnish, or crushed and made into a paste, as in pesto.

Fettuccine alla salsa di limone

Fettuccine with lemon sauce

1 pound fettuccine	3 tablespoons butter
1 cup medium cream	4 tablespoons Parmesan cheese, grated
1 lemon skin, grated	1/8 teaspoon white pepper
1 teaspoon lemon juice	pinch nutmeg
1 shot vodka	pinch salt

Combine cream, butter, nutmeg, salt, and white pepper in sauce pan or double boiler.
When the mixture is warm, mix in the lemon gratings.
Add the vodka and cook over low heat for about 10 minutes.
Cook and strain pasta, saving 1 tablespoon pasta water.
Pour pasta in heated serving dish. Add sauce and mix well.
Add 1 tablespoon of pasta water, lemon juice, and Parmesan. Mix thoroughly.

WINES: Frascati, Orvieto bianco, Tocai

ALTERNATE PASTA: Vermicelli, Trenette, Linguine

Spaghetti al limone

Spaghetti with lemon

1 pound spaghetti
rind of 2 lemons, grated
3/4 cup cooked ham, diced finely
1 egg yolk, beaten
3 tablespoons Parmesan cheese, grated
1/2 cup medium cream

1 tablespoon onion, finely chopped
2 teaspoons parsley, finely chopped
2 tablespoons olive oil
2 tablespoons butter
salt and pepper

In a large skillet, sauté onion in butter and oil.
Add ham and continue cooking over low heat for 7–10 minutes.
Remove from heat, add cream, lemon rind, and beaten egg yolk.
Mix well after each addition. Salt and pepper to taste.
Prepare pasta, strain, but save a few tablespoons of pasta water.
Place pasta in heated serving bowl. Mix in Parmesan and sauce, with the reserved pasta water.
Top each serving with chopped parsley.

WINES: Tocai, Orvieto bianco, Corvo bianco, Bianco di Custoza

ALTERNATE PASTA: Vermicelli, Trenette, Linguine

Fettuccine all'agretta

Fettuccine with lemon juice

1 pound fettuccine
6 tablespoons butter
2 egg yolks, at room temperature
2 tablespoons fresh lemon juice

1/3 cup Parmesan cheese, grated
1/8 teaspoon white pepper
pinch of salt

While pasta is cooking, lightly beat 2 egg yolks in serving bowl.
Add in lemon juice and set aside. Melt butter in small skillet, salt and pepper, stir, and also set aside.
Quickly drain pasta cooked al dente and combine in bowl with egg yolks.
Mix quickly so that egg congeals on pasta.
Add melted butter and cheese and mix again.

WINES: Tocai, Orvieto bianco, Corvo bianco

ALTERNATE PASTA: Spaghetti, Vermicelli, Trenette, Linguine

Tagliatelle ai quattro formaggi

Tagliatelle with four cheeses

1 pound tagliatelle
2/3 cup gouda cheese, grated
2/3 cup swiss cheese, grated
1/2 cup mozzarella cheese, grated

2/3 cup Parmesan cheese, grated
5 tablespoons butter, at room temperature
2 tablespoons fresh parsley, chopped
white pepper

Combine all cheeses, except Parmesan, in large bowl and set aside at room temperature.
Cook pasta, strain, and place in a warm serving dish.
Mix in cheeses which will melt on the hot pasta.
Mix in butter, broken up into small pieces to facilitate melting.
Season with white pepper and mix again.
Top each serving with Parmesan and parsley. Serve immediately.

WINES: Tocai, Pinot grigio, Orvieto bianco, Bianco delle Cinque Terre

ALTERNATE PASTA: Fettuccine, Linguine

Spaghetti con mozzarella

Spaghetti with mozzarella

1 pound spaghetti
1/2 pound fresh mozzarella, cut in small cubes
1½ cups tomatoes, peeled, cut in pieces
4 anchovie fillets, finely chopped
2 tablespoons capers, well rinsed

green olives, pitted, no pimiento,
  6 per person
1 small onion, finely chopped
1/3 cup olive oil
3 fresh basil leaves
freshly ground pepper

In a medium skillet, sauté onion in oil. Add tomatoes and simmer for about 20 minutes.
Season with basil and pepper. Prepare pasta and place in heated serving bowl.
Add mozzarella and tomato sauce, and toss rapidly.
Mix in capers, anchovies and olives. Serve immediately.

WINES: Soave, Orvieto bianco

ALTERNATE PASTA: Linguine, Trenette, Vermicelli

At one time, soft mozzarella cheese was obtained exclusively from central and southern regions of Italy, where it was made from buffalo milk.
The classic mozzarella comes from the Maremma region and is called "mozzarella di bufala."
Today, fresh mozzarella, which is used for pizza, is also made in northern Italy from cow's milk.
This cheese also comes smoked and is used in pasta al forno (baked in the oven) dishes, such as gnocchi.

A firmer mozzarella, yellowish in color, is also available; it is typically sliced and fried on a griddle, then eaten as a tasty appetizer.

Rigatoni al gorgonzola

Rigatoni with gorgonzola

1 pound rigatoni
1 cup gorgonzola cheese, crumbled
1/2 cup light cream

2 tablespoons butter
2 tablespoons fresh parsley, chopped
white pepper

Melt butter in a small sauce pan. Add cream and gorgonzola.
Pepper to taste. Cook over medium heat until cheese is mostly melted and sauce thickens.
Stir continuously. Add sauce to cooked and strained pasta and mix well.
Top with sprinkling of parsley.

WINES: Rosato del Piave, Riviera rosato, Rosé

ALTERNATE PASTA: Ziti corti, All Penne

Penne della nonna Carmela

Grandma Carmela's Penne

1 pound penne
3½ cups tomatoes, peeled and crushed
1 medium onion, sliced
1 medium eggplant
olive oil

2 tablespoons butter
6–8 fresh basil leaves
1/3 cup ricotta cheese, at room temperature
salt and black pepper

In a large skillet, sauté sliced onion in oil and butter until onion is softened.
When onion is slightly golden, add tomatoes, basil, and a dash of black pepper.
Simmer over low heat for 15–20 minutes until sauce thickens.
In the meantime, prepare eggplant by removing skins and ends.
Place eggplant on its side and cut one-half-inch slices and fry in hot oil.
When tender, remove eggplant from oil and drain well on paper towels. Salt lightly.
Cut eggplant into two-inch long strips, place in bowl and cover to keep warm.
Boil pasta, drain, and then dress with ricotta and sauce. Gently fold in eggplant pieces.

WINES: Cirò rosso, Pollino rosso, Chianti Gallo Nero, Gattinara

ALTERNATE PASTA: Ziti corti, Rigatoni

This recipe originated in Calabria, where ricotta and eggplant are combined in many recipes.
To keep the eggplant from absorbing too much oil, fry it over low heat, and only add oil as required.

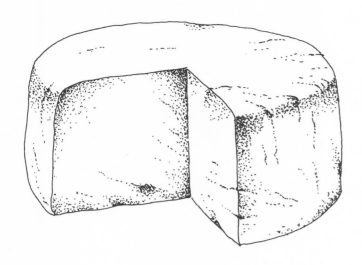

Bucatini con la ricotta

Bucatini with ricotta

1 pound bucatini
3/4 cup ricotta cheese, at room temperature
3 tablespoons melted butter

3 tablespoons heavy cream
2 tablespoons Parmesan cheese, grated

In a large bowl combine ricotta, butter and cream.
Cook pasta al dente, strain, but save at least 1 tablespoon of pasta water.
Add pasta to cheese mixture and thin with pasta water.
Top off with Parmesan and mix well.

WINES: Soave, Prosecco di Valdobbiadene

ALTERNATE PASTA: Perciatelli, Mezzani lunghi, Fusilli

Ricotta is a soft, sweet cheese that resembles cottage cheese.
It is made from a by-product of other cheeses: the left-over whey.
"Ricotta," which means recooked, gets its name because it is cooked twice.
It can be made either with cow's milk or sheep's milk, but the product of sheep's milk is tastier.
Ricotta is used in many pasta dishes in southern Italy, usually in white sauces or tomato sauces.

Rigatoni rustici alla Diana

Rigatoni Diana

1 pound rigatoni
1/2 pound sausage, skins removed
1/2 pound ricotta cheese, pressed through
  a strainer
1/2 cup light cream

1/4 cup Romano cheese, grated
1/2 cup water
1 teaspoon parsley, finely chopped
salt and pepper

Crumble sausage in small sauce pan, add just enough water to cover, and boil until sausage is fully cooked.
Strain off cooking water into large bowl. Set sausage aside.
Add ricotta to cooking water in bowl, then add fresh pepper, salt and parsley. Mix well.
Cook pasta al dente, strain and pour into ricotta mixture.
Mix well. Add sausage, Romano, and cream, and toss gently.

WINES: Merlot, Bardolino, Chiaretto

ALTERNATE PASTA: Ziti corti, All Penne

Pasta Fantasia

Fettuccine with champagne

12 ounces egg fettuccine
1 small onion, finely chopped
4 tablespoons butter

2 cups beef broth
2 cups dry champagne, pink or white
1/2 cup Parmesan cheese, grated

In a large skillet, sauté onion in butter until softened, but not browned.
Add broth and allow to cook over medium heat for 3–5 minutes.
Meanwhile, cook pasta in boiling water until half done, strain, then add to broth mixture.
Stirring constantly, add the champagne and continue cooking until most of the liquid has been absorbed and fettuccine is cooked al dente.
Mix in Parmesan and serve immediately.

WINES: Pinot grigio, Prosecco di Valdobbiadene, Corvo bianco or Champagne

ALTERNATE PASTA: Egg-Tagliatelle, egg-Tagliolini

In Italy, champagne is often used to cook rice, which absorbs much of the champagne's delicate flavor.
If soft-egg pasta is partially cooked, drained, and then simmered in champagne,
it will, happily, also absorb the flavor.
The key is to know when to take the pasta from the water and put in the champagne, so as not to overcook it.
And it must be eaten immediately, because the champagne fragrance tends to evaporate rapidly.
This recipe was invented by my father, and it is a tribute to a great cook.

Penne al brandy

Penne with Brandy

1 pound penne
1 small onion, finely chopped
3 tablespoons olive oil
1/2 cup brandy

2 cups tomatoes, peeled, cut in pieces
1/4 cup Parmesan cheese, grated
salt and pepper

Sauté onion in oil until golden. Add brandy, and simmer for 2−3 minutes.
Add the tomatoes, salt and pepper, and cook over medium heat until sauce thickens slightly.
Pour over pasta cooked al dente and top with Parmesan.

WINES: Soave, Tocai, Orvieto bianco

ALTERNATE PASTA: All Penne

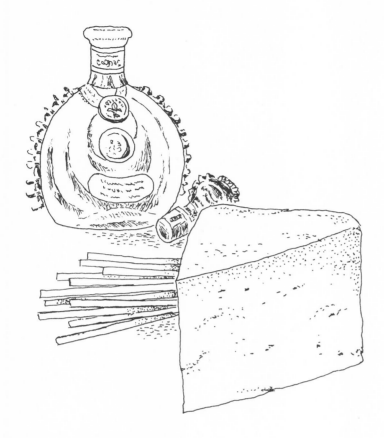

Spaghetti al cognac

Spaghetti with cognac

1 pound spaghetti
1/2 cup cognac
1/3 cup Parmesan cheese, grated

6 tablespoons butter
1/8 teaspoon pepper
dash salt

Boil spaghetti in salted water.
Five minutes before draining, melt butter in a large skillet over low heat and add salt and pepper.
Raise heat to medium and pour in cognac. Cover and simmer for 2−3 minutes.
Drain pasta and place in serving bowl. Top with sauce and mix.
Add grated cheese, mix again and serve immediately.

WINES: Pinot grigio, Soave, Verdicchio

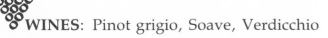

ALTERNATE PASTA: Trenette, Linguine, Fettuccine, All Penne

Penne alla vodka

Penne with vodka

1 pound penne
1/2 cup vodka
1/2 cup light cream
1/3 cup smoked ham, diced

1/2 cup tomatoes, peeled and crushed
1/2 cup Parmesan cheese, grated
3 tablespoons olive oil
pinch white pepper

In a medium skillet, sauté ham in oil for 3 minutes.
Reduce heat to medium-low. Add vodka and let evaporate.
Add crushed tomatoes and cream, and stir constantly until well-blended.
Season with pepper and cook covered over low heat for 2 minutes.
Cook pasta al dente, mix in sauce, and top with Parmesan.

WINES: Soave, Tocai, Orvieto bianco

ALTERNATE PASTA: Mezzi Siti, Trenette, All Penne

Spaghetti alla marinara

Spaghetti with marinara sauce

1 pound spaghetti
2 cups ripe fresh plum tomatoes, cored,
   cut in pieces
1 small onion, finely chopped
8 fresh basil leaves

2 garlic cloves
1/4 cup parsley, chopped
1/3 cup olive oil
salt and pepper

In a large skillet, sauté onion and garlic in olive oil.
Add basil leaves, and continue cooking for 2 minutes.
Mix in tomatoes, and season with salt and pepper.
Simmer for 15 minutes. Pour sauce over pasta cooked al dente.
Garnish with parsley.

WINES: Pinot grigio, Verdicchio

ALTERNATE PASTA: Linguine, Vermicelli, Spaghettini

Spaghetti ca pommarola 'n coppa

Spaghetti with tomatoes on top

1 pound spaghetti
3 cups ripe, fresh plum tomatoes
16 fresh basil leaves

8 tablespoons olive oil
salt

Wash, dry, core, and cut tomatoes lengthwise in eighths.
Heat oil in a large skillet. Add in tomatoes and 8 basil leaves.
Salt to taste. Simmer tomatoes for 3 minutes.
Pour sauce over pasta cooked al dente and mix thoroughly.
Top with remaining basil leaves.

WINES: Rosé, Chiaretto, Biancolella

ALTERNATE PASTA: Vermicelli, Linguine, Spaghettini

This classic tomato sauce originated in Naples, where the Neapolitans—blessed by a mild climate, marine breezes, and spring waters—grow the best tomatoes in Italy.
Known as "San Marzano," this tomato, combined with fresh basil leaves and olive oil, makes a superior sauce.
"Pommarola 'n coppa" means "tomatoes on top," or on top of pasta, a simple and delicious dish.

Spaghetti con salsa a crudo

Spaghetti with uncooked sauce

1 pound spaghetti
6 tablespoons olive oil
3 cups ripe fresh plum tomatoes, cored,
   cut in pieces

2 garlic cloves
10 fresh basil leaves
salt

This sauce requires no cooking, hence the word *"crudo"* which means raw.
While pasta is cooking, combine oil, tomatoes, and basil leaves in serving bowl.
When pasta is cooked, strain, and mix into serving bowl.
Salt to taste, and serve.
Ingredients can be combined well in advance and allowed to steep for enhanced flavor.

WINES: Soave, Pinot grigio, Orvieto bianco

ALTERNATE PASTA: Vermicelli, Trenette, Linguine

Pennette con broccoli

Pennette with broccoli

1 pound pennette
1/2 pound boiled broccoli, cut in pieces
1 clove garlic

4 tablespoons olive oil
1 peperoncino or hot red pepper, crushed

In a large skillet, sauté garlic and peperoncino (or hot pepper) in oil.
When garlic is light brown, add broccoli pieces and mix well.
Serve over pasta cooked al dente.

WINES: Valpolicella, Chianti classico, Cabernet

ALTERNATE PASTA: All Penne

Although this recipe calls for broccoli, any vegetable in the broccoli family, such as cauliflower, can be substituted. This dish originated in the low mountain regions of central Italy, where broccoli grows abundantly.

Penne con asparagi

Penne with asparagus

1 pound penne
2 pounds fresh asparagus
4 ounces butter

1/2 cup Parmesan cheese, grated
black pepper

Clean and wash asparagus, and boil in salted water for 4 minutes.
After straining, cut off and place tips in a medium skillet with 2 ounces butter.
Sauté for 5–6 minutes. Pepper lightly.
Cook penne al dente, strain, and place in heated serving dish.
Add asparagus tips, remaining butter cut in small pieces, and grated Parmesan. Mix well.

WINES: Tocai, Bianco di Custoza, Frascati

ALTERNATE PASTA: All Penne, Rigatoni, Ziti corti

Linguine con spinaci e besciamella

Linguine with spinach and besciamella

1 pound linguine
1/2 cup walnut meats, finely chopped
1 pound spinach leaves, washed thoroughly

1/4 teaspoon nutmeg
1/3 cup Parmesan cheese, grated
1/8 teaspoon salt

Besciamella sauce

1 1/4 cup warm milk
3 tablespoons butter

4 tablespoons flour

Cook spinach and drain, saving 2 tablespoons of liquid.
Finely chop the spinach and set aside.
Prepare besciamella sauce in a small sauce pan or double boiler; melt butter over low heat and add a little flour at a time to form paste. While still on low heat add warm milk slowly until a creamy consistency is formed.
Mix in the spinach liquid. Season with salt and nutmeg and mix well.
In a bowl, gently mix the besciamella sauce, spinach, and nuts.
Dress cooked linguine with sauce and garnish with Parmesan.

WINES: Chiaretto, Rosé, Orvieto bianco

ALTERNATE PASTA: Spaghetti, Vermicelli, Trenette, Fettuccine

Besciamella sauce can be used as a flavoring or as a base for many pasta sauces.
A creamy, white sauce that originated in Florence, besciamella was first brought to France by Catherine de' Medici, who married the heir to the French throne in 1533.
Today, French cooks call this sauce bêchamel.
In Italy, besciamella is served over pasta or cooked vegetables, or it is combined with specific tomato sauces to make them creamier and more palatable.

Fusilli alla Carolina

Fusilli Carolina

1 pound fusilli
1 cup zucchini, rinsed and diced
1/2 cup peas, fresh
1/2 cup tender asparagus tips
1/2 cup young string beans
2 cups plum tomatoes, peeled

1/4 cup onion, finely chopped
1/2 cup dry wine
1¾ cups beef broth
1/3 cup Parmesan, grated
5 tablespoons olive oil
salt and pepper

Prepare string beans by washing them and removing ends; cut into one-inch pieces.
Wash asparagus and cut-off tips. Boil string beans and asparagus tips in lightly salted water until cooked; set aside.
In a large skillet, sauté onion in olive oil until onion softens, then remove it.
In same oil, sauté zucchini and remove; in same oil, sauté peas.
When peas are cooked, place the onions and zucchini back into the skillet, and add asparagus and string beans.
Pour in wine and simmer until evaporated; pour in 3/4 cups of beef broth and simmer for about 15 minutes or until sauce condenses.
Add tomatoes, simmer for 10 minutes, stirring carefully.
Salt and pepper to taste. Add remaining broth and simmer until desired consistency is reached.
Pour sauce over cooked pasta, and top with grated Parmesan.

WINES: Bianco di Custoza, Orvieto bianco, Tocai

ALTERNATE PASTA: Eliche, All Penne

The Italian countryside boasts a rich variety of vegetables—the pride of Italy.
The vegetables that can be used in this recipe are practically limitless, and depend only on the preference and imagination of the cook.

Spaghetti con sugo di melanzane

Spaghetti with eggplant

1 pound spaghetti
1 garlic clove
1 medium eggplant
1 tablespoon onion, chopped
2 cups tomatoes, peeled and crushed

5 fresh basil leaves
1/3 cup Parmesan cheese, grated
3 tablespoons olive oil
salt and pepper

In a large skillet, sauté garlic and onion in olive oil.
Add tomatoes, salt and pepper, and simmer for 20 minutes.
Add a little water if needed. Add fresh basil leaves and continue cooking.
In the meantime, remove ends of eggplant leaving skin on, and slice length-wise, one-half inch thick. Fry in hot oil placing eggplant on absorbent paper to drain.
Salt slightly. Cut eggplant into finger-like strips.
Add cooked eggplant to sauce and simmer 3–4 more minutes.
Pour sauce over pasta and top with Parmesan.

WINES: Merlot, Bardolino, Raboso

ALTERNATE PASTA: Vermicelli, Perciatelli, Bucatini

Eggplant is widely used in southern Italy.
Basilicata, Puglie, Calabria, and Sicilia all boast special recipes for this vegetable.
A favorite method of preparing eggplant, besides frying, is to slice it and spread a few drops of oil on each side, then bake it on an oven griddle until browned on both sides.
This method keeps the eggplant from absorbing too much oil, while it locks in flavor.

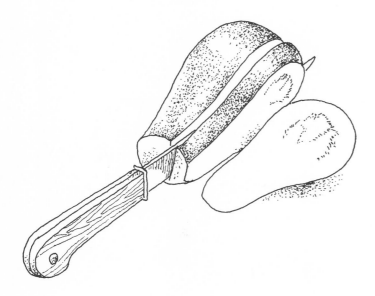

Penne all'Ilaria

Penne Ilaria

1 pound penne
1 small eggplant
1/4 cup mozzarella cheese, cubed
2 cups tomatoes, peeled, cut in pieces
1/3 cup Romano cheese, grated

16 fresh basil leaves, medium-sized
2 tablespoons onion, finely chopped
5 tablespoons olive oil
salt and pepper

Wash eggplant and remove ends but leave skin on.
Cut into one-quarter inch thick slices and fry in oil.
Place on absorbent paper to drain. Cut into pieces, set aside.
In a large skillet, sauté onions until softened. Add in tomatoes, salt and pepper, and simmer for 10−15 minutes.
Cook pasta, drain, and add to skillet.
Gently fold in the eggplant pieces, basil leaves and the mozzarella.
Mix until mozzarella softens. Top with Romano, and serve.

WINES: Rosato del Veneto, Chiaretto, Rosatello

ALTERNATE PASTA: All Penne

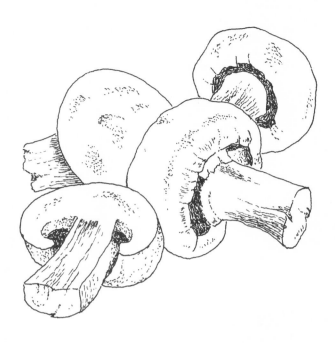

Penne con funghi e panna

Penne with mushrooms and cream

1 pound penne
3/4 pound mushrooms, cleaned, sliced
4 tablespoons butter
2 tablespoons olive oil
1 shot brandy

1 garlic clove
1/2 cup light cream, at room temperature
1/2 cup Parmesan cheese, grated
salt and pepper

In a large skillet sauté garlic in oil and 2 tablespoons of butter until golden.
Remove garlic and add mushrooms, brandy, salt and pepper, and simmer for 5−10 minutes until the brandy evaporates.
Reduce heat to low. Add cream and stir gently.
Add remaining butter to cooked pasta and mix well. Add sauce and mix gently.
Top with grated Parmesan. Serve immediately.

WINES: Rosé, Bardolino, Merlot

ALTERNATE PASTA: Eliche, Rigatoni, Fusilli

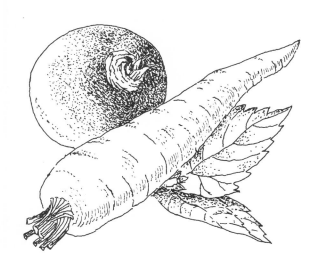

Penne alla contadina

Penne of the peasants

1 pound penne
2 cups tomatoes, peeled and cut in pieces
2 celery stalks, chopped
1 carrot, chopped
1 onion, finely chopped
1 turnip, chopped

4 tablespoons butter
1/3 cup Parmesan cheese, grated
basil
thyme
salt and pepper

Melt butter in a large skillet, add tomatoes and other vegetables.
Season with salt, pepper, thyme, and basil.
Cover and simmer over medium-low heat for about 30 minutes.
If sauce becomes too dry, pour in a little water.
Cook pasta, drain, and place in heated serving dish.
Mix in sauce and top with grated Parmesan.

WINES: Pinot grigio, Corvo bianco, Prosecco di Valdobbiadene

ALTERNATE PASTA: All Penne

Spaghetti alla Piccirì

Spaghetti with minced mushrooms

1 pound spaghetti	3 pinches hot cayenne pepper
2 cups mushrooms, cleaned and minced	1/2 cup dry white wine
7 tablespoons olive oil	2 tablespoons butter
5 garlic cloves, halved	salt

In a large skillet, sauté garlic in oil until golden brown.
Remove garlic and add cayenne pepper.
In same pan, sauté mushrooms for about 5 minutes.
Pour in wine and simmer until wine evaporates. Season with salt.
Cook pasta al dente and strain.
Place pasta in serving platter with butter cut in small pieces and mix rapidly.
Combine sauce and mix thoroughly.

WINES: Rapitalà, Pinot grigio, Bianco delle Cinque Terre, Orvieto bianco

ALTERNATE PASTA: Linguine, Vermicelli, Trenette

Legend has it that this recipe was invented by a cook from Calabria as a tribute to his petite wife, who loved mushrooms.
"Picciri," which means "small," requires the mushrooms to be minced into tiny pieces and simmered in wine. The cayenne pepper is added to bring out the zest of this recipe.

Fettuccine Favolose

Fabulous Fettuccine

1 pound egg-fettuccine
1/3 cup capers
1/8 teaspoon crushed red pepper
black and green olives with pimiento, pitted,
   10 per person
1½ cups tomatoes, peeled
1 medium onion, finely chopped

3 tablespoons olive oil
3 tablespoons butter
1/3 cup fresh parsley, finely chopped
12 fresh basil leaves
salt

In a medium skillet, sauté onions and parsley in oil and butter until onion turns golden.
Add tomatoes and 6 leaves of basil, and break up tomatoes with a fork.
Continue cooking over medium-low heat for about 5 minutes.
Cook pasta, strain, and place in a heated serving bowl.
Quickly add sauce, olives, capers, and hot pepper.
Mix well, serve the remaining fresh basil leaves as garnish.

WINES: Merlot, Bardolino

ALTERNATE PASTA: egg-Tagliatelle

Trenette con vitello e asparagi

Trenette with veal and asparagus

1 pound trenette	1 cup dry white wine
1 pound tender fresh asparagus	6 tablespoons butter
1/8 pound ground veal	1 small onion, chopped
1½ cups light cream	salt and pepper

Cut off asparagus tips and wash them. In a large skillet, lightly sauté asparagus tips in butter along with chopped onion.
Add veal; when cooked, add wine, and simmer for 2 or 3 minutes, stirring occasionally.
Season with salt and pepper. Lower heat and add cream.
When sauce has reduced a little and is of consistency desired, pour over pasta cooked al dente. Mix thoroughly.

WINES: Rosé, Chiaretto

ALTERNATE PASTA: Fettuccine, Spaghetti, Vermicelli

Penne alla zucca

Penne with fresh pumpkin

1 pound penne
3 cups fresh pumpkin pulp, cut in cubes
1/4 cup onion, minced
2 strips bacon, diced
1/4 cup Parmesan cheese, grated

3/4 cup beef broth
4 tablespoons butter
1 tablespoon olive oil
1 tablespoon parsley, finely chopped
salt and pepper

In a large skillet, sauté onion in oil and 2 tablespoons of butter.
Add bacon and pumpkin and stir. Pour in beef broth, cover, and simmer for 20 minutes.
Remove cover and continue cooking until broth nearly evaporates. Salt and pepper to taste.
Stir occasionally.
Cook pasta al dente, strain, and place in pan with sauce. Add remaining butter, cut in small pieces.
Mix thoroughly but gently.
Place in serving dish and mix in grated Parmesan. Top with parsley.

WINES: Rosé, Bardolino, Merlot

ALTERNATE PASTA: Ziti corti, Rigatoni

Pumpkins are not usually associated with Italian food, but they are very popular in Italy, as are other ghourds such as butternut and acorn squash. Frequently combined with other vegetables to make pasta sauce, pumpkins are also used in hot and cold soups.

Fettuccine con zucchini

Fettuccine with zucchini

1 pound fettuccine
1 pound zucchini, rinsed and cubed
5 strips bacon, diced
1/3 cup Parmesan cheese, grated

3 tablespoons butter
3 fresh basil leaves
salt and white pepper

In a large skillet, sauté zucchini in melted butter.
When half cooked, add bacon, basil leaves, and salt and pepper to taste.
Cook bacon thoroughly but not crispy. Pour over cooked pasta and mix in Parmesan.

WINES: Rosé, Chiaretto

ALTERNATE PASTA: Tagliatelle, Linguine

Fettuccine del Principe

Fettuccine for a Prince

1 pound fettuccine
1 pound cauliflower, washed
1 cup mozzarella, cubed
1 cup smoked ham, diced or cut in strips
1 cup mortadella, diced or cut in strips

1/3 cup Parmesan cheese, grated
3 tablespoons butter
3 tablespoons olive oil
1 garlic clove, whole
salt and freshly ground pepper

In a large uncovered pot, boil cauliflower for 15 minutes.
In a large skillet, sauté garlic in butter and olive oil until golden brown. Remove garlic.
Remove cauliflower from boiling water, and cook fettuccine in same water.
Cut cooked cauliflower into small pieces and add to skillet.
Cook over low heat for about 5 minutes, stirring occasionally.
Add ham and mortadella. Drain pasta when cooked al dente and mix with sauce.
Cook over high heat for one minute and stir. Lower heat. Add mozzarella and Parmesan.
Stir briskly until cheeses melt slightly and season with freshly ground pepper.

WINES: Merlot, Bardolino, Corvo rosso

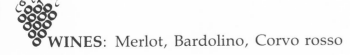

ALTERNATE PASTA: Spaghetti, Vermicelli, Trenette, Tagliatelle

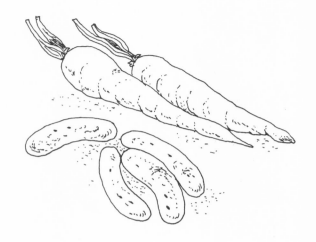

Rigatoni alle carote

Rigatoni with carrots

1 pound rigatoni
2 carrots, finely chopped
1 cup tomatoes, peeled, cut in pieces
1/4 pound sausage, skin removed
1 small onion, finely chopped

1/4 cup Parmesan cheese, grated
pinch of marjoram
5 tablespoons olive oil
3 tablespoons beef broth
salt and pepper

In a large skillet, sauté onion until golden in olive oil.
Add carrots and cook, stirring for 5 minutes over medium heat.
Add sausage and cook until browned.
Mix in tomatoes, salt and pepper; cook for 30 minutes over low heat.
Pour in broth during the cooking process to keep sauce from becoming too thick.
When carrots are well softened, remove skillet from heat and stir in a pinch of marjoram.
Place cooked pasta in heated serving dish and top with prepared sauce.
Serve sprinkled with grated Parmesan.

WINES: Orvieto bianco, Frascati, Pinot grigio

ALTERNATE PASTA: Ziti, Mezzi Ziti, Mezzani

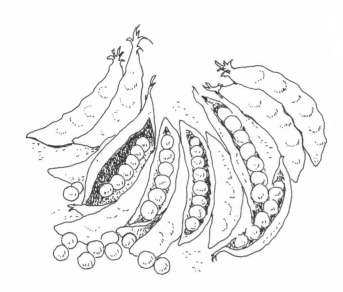

Farfalle con piselli

Farfalle with peas

1 pound farfalle
1 pound fresh peas, shelled
1/8 pound cooked ham, diced
3/4 cup light cream, at room temperature
1 small onion, chopped

4 tablespoons butter
2 tablespoons olive oil
4 tablespoons Parmesan cheese, grated
1 cup beef broth

In a large skillet, sauté onion in 2 tablespoons butter and 2 tablespoons oil.
When onion turns golden, add peas and diced ham.
Cook for 7−10 minutes over medium heat stirring constantly.
Add 1/2 cup broth and simmer for 10 minutes. If sauce becomes too dry, add additional broth.
Cook pasta al dente, strain, and place in heated serving dish.
Add cheese and remaining butter.
Toss gently, then dress with sauce and cream. Mix again.

WINES: Pinot grigio, Corvo bianco, Prosecco di Valdobbiadene

ALTERNATE PASTA: Pennette, Ditali, Conchigliette

Fettuccine Arcobaleno

Rainbow fettuccine

1 pound fettuccine
1 pound peppers: red, green and yellow
2 strips bacon, diced

2 tablespoons butter
3 garlic cloves
salt and pepper

In a pot, parboil whole peppers until soft. Remove the core and seeds and slice lengthwise into strips.
In a large skillet, lightly brown bacon and garlic in butter.
Add peppers to bacon mixture and cook for 3–5 minutes over low heat, stirring frequently. Remove garlic cloves, and season with salt and pepper. Pour over pasta cooked al dente, and toss gently.

WINES: Valpolicella, Cabernet

ALTERNATE PASTA: Tagliatelle, Linguine

This recipe originated in Basilicata, a province in southern Italy, where colorful dishes are the rule. With their vast array of lush vegetables, southern Italian cooks have little difficulty living up to the local proverb: "Let the mouth have its taste, but let the eye have its part."

Fettuccine Trastevere

Fettuccine from Trastevere

1 pound fettuccine
3 artichokes, very tender
1 cup beef broth
juice of 1/2 lemon
2 tablespoons olive oil
1 small onion, finely chopped

1/3 cup smoked ham, finely chopped
2 tablespoons butter
1/2 cup dry white wine
1/2 cup light cream
1/4 cup Parmesan cheese, grated
salt and pepper

Wash artichokes, trim bottoms, and remove outer leaves until only those tender leaves closest to the heart remain.
Cut in half and remove hay. Cut into strips or slices and place in water with a few drops of lemon juice.
In a large skillet, sauté onion and ham in oil and butter.
Strain, rinse and dry artichoke slices, and place in skillet cooking over medium high heat for several minutes.
Pour in white wine. When wine has evaporated, add 1/2 cup broth and continue cooking for about 30 minutes over a moderate heat, adding broth until the artichokes are tender.
Lower heat, salt and pepper, and mix in cream.
Simmer for a few minutes. Pour sauce over pasta cooked al dente.
Top with grated Parmesan.

WINES: Rosé, Chiaretto

ALTERNATE PASTA: Linguine, Vermicelli, Perciatelli, Spaghettini

"Trastevere" means "on the other side of the Tiber" and refers to a small section of Rome extending along the Tiber River. In many ways, Trastevere is still largely rooted in the past; its residents take great pride in their magnificent neighborhood and their glorious heritage. This recipe, in the spirit of ancient Rome, reflects that feeling.

Penne al sugo di carciofi

Penne with artichoke sauce

1 pound penne
1 cup tomatoes, peeled
4 artichoke hearts, or 6 baby artichokes
3 slices bacon, diced
1 medium onion, chopped

1/4 cup fresh parsley, chopped
1 garlic clove, whole
1/3 cup olive oil
1/3 cup Parmesan cheese, grated
salt and freshly ground black pepper

Prepare each artichoke by removing outer leaves until the soft heart is exposed.
Cut in quarters, remove hay, and soak in water with a few drops of lemon juice until they are to be placed in boiling water.
In a large skillet, sauté onion and parsley in olive oil.
Add diced bacon and garlic, and remove garlic when golden brown.
Add tomatoes breaking them up with a wooden spoon.
Salt and pepper to taste. Cook for 5 minutes over medium-high heat, stirring constantly.
Rinse artichokes and boil them in the same water you will use for the pasta.
When nearly cooked, remove artichokes with strainer and add pasta in the same water.
A few minutes before pasta is cooked al dente, place artichokes back in boiling water with pasta.
Drain artichokes and pasta together and dress with prepared sauce.
Top with Parmesan and a dash of freshly ground black pepper.

WINES: Rosé, Chiaretto

ALTERNATE PASTA: Ziti corti, Rigatoni

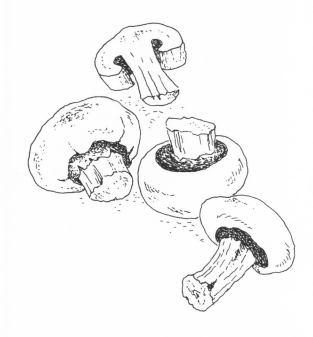

Rigatoni al sugo di funghi

Rigatoni with mushroom sauce

1 pound rigatoni
1/3 cup cooked ham, diced
3/4 pound mushrooms, cleaned and sliced
2 garlic cloves, whole

1/2 cup olive oil
1/2 cup beef broth
1 tablespoon parsley, chopped
salt and black pepper

Place ham, garlic, and oil in a large skillet and cook over medium heat until ham begins to brown but not become crispy.
Add mushrooms, and season with salt and pepper.
Remove garlic. Continue cooking for about 5 minutes, stirring continuously.
Pour in broth, cover the pan, and cook for 8–10 minutes.
Remove the cover, add parsley and cook an additional 5 minutes. Sauce should be light, not thick.
Pour sauce over pasta cooked al dente.

WINES: Rosato del Veneto, Chiaretto

ALTERNATE PASTA: All Penne

Spaghetti con brio

Spaghetti with spirit

1 pound spaghetti
1 pound fresh mushrooms, cleaned and sliced
5 tablespoons butter
1 garlic clove, whole
1 tablespoon parsley, finely chopped
5 strips bacon, finely chopped

1/3 cup beef broth
2 tablespoons olive oil
1 small onion, finely chopped
1 cup tomatoes, peeled, cut in pieces
4 tablespoons Parmesan cheese, grated
1/3 cup light cream

In a large skillet, sauté mushrooms and garlic in 2 tablespoons butter.
Pour in heated broth and cook over low heat for one minute.
Salt and pepper. Remove garlic, and add parsley.
In a separate skillet, sauté bacon and onion in 2 tablespoons of oil.
Mix in tomatoes and cook over a moderate flame for 8−10 minutes, stirring frequently.
Cook pasta, drain, and place in warm serving bowl.
Add cream, remaining portions of butter, and Parmesan to pasta.
Toss gently. Add bacon mixture and mix well.
Top with mushrooms, and serve immediately.

WINES: Merlot, Bardolino, Raboso, Chianti classico

ALTERNATE PASTA: Vermicelli, Bucatini, Spaghettini

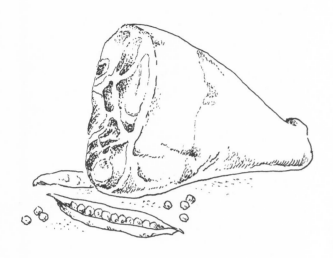

Spaghetti ai tre sapori

Spaghetti with three flavors

1 pound spaghetti
1/2 pound fresh mushrooms, cleaned, sliced
1/4 pound smoked ham, diced
4 tablespoons fresh peas, shelled

3/4 cup beef broth
4 tablespoons butter
4 tablespoons Parmesan cheese, grated
dash ground pepper

In a large skillet, sauté mushrooms in butter for 2 minutes.
Add ham, peas, and broth. Cover and simmer over low heat for 15 minutes.
Add pepper, and stir occasionally. Pour sauce over pasta, cooked al dente, and top with Parmesan.

WINES: Chiaretto, Rosé

ALTERNATE PASTA: Spaghettini, Vermicelli, Bucatini

Vermicelli a modo mio

Vermicelli my style

1 pound vermicelli
3 cups diced eggplant, with skin on
1 sweet pepper, red or green
15–20 green olives, pitted, no pimento
2 anchovie fillets, finely chopped
1 heaping tablespoon capers

3 fresh basil leaves
4 tablespoons olive oil
1 garlic clove, chopped
3½ cups tomatoes, peeled and crushed
salt and pepper

Parboil whole pepper for a few minutes until soft.
In a large skillet, sauté garlic in oil, add tomatoes and eggplant and cook until eggplant is tender, about 15 minutes.
Core and slice pepper lengthwise into strips, removing seeds, and add to sauce.
Mix in olives, capers, and basil leaves, then add anchovie fillets.
Cover and cook until olives become tender.
Combine sauce with pasta cooked al dente and serve with plenty of black pepper.

WINES: Merlot, Corvo rosso

ALTERNATE PASTA: Spaghetti, Bucatini, Perciatelli, All Penne

Anchovies, like sardines, are a type of bluefish.
They swim in large schools, have silver, green, and blue stripes, and can grow to as much as ten inches long.
Most people think of anchovies as spicey, salty fish because they are packed in salt and oil, but they have a more delicate flavor when eaten fresh.
Anchovies are caught in the Mediterranean all year long and are very popular in Italy.
Traditionally, Italian fish markets feature anchovies every Tuesday and Friday.

Spaghetti con olive nere

Spaghetti with black olives

1 pound spaghetti
3/4 cup whole tomatoes
4 tablespoons olive oil
2 garlic cloves, whole

2 pinches crushed hot red pepper
4 anchovie fillets
10 black grecian olives, pitted and minced

Sauté garlic in oil until slightly golden, and remove garlic.
Add crushed pepper and anchovie fillets, breaking the fillets up with a wooden spoon until blended.
Stir in tomatoes, and add minced olives, simmer for two minutes. Serve over cooked pasta.

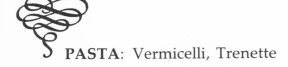

WINES: Orvieto bianco, Marino, Pinot grigio

PASTA: Vermicelli, Trenette

Tagliatelle al prosciutto e piselli

Tagliatelle with prosciutto and peas

1 pound tagliatelle
1/4 pound prosciutto, finely chopped
1/2 pound shelled fresh peas
1/3 cup light cream
1/3 cup of water
1 small onion, finely chopped

3 tablespoons butter
1 tablespoon olive oil
1 tablespoon fresh parsley, minced
2 tablespoons Parmesan cheese, grated
salt and pepper

In a large skillet, lightly sauté onion in butter and oil.
Add prosciutto. When the prosciutto is browned, add peas, water, and stir.
Cover and cook over medium heat until peas are softened.
Season with salt and pepper. Add parsley and cream.
Simmer for a few minutes. Pour sauce over pasta cooked al dente and serve with Parmesan.

WINES: Bardolino, Merlot, Chianti classico

ALTERNATE PASTA: Fettuccine, egg-Tagliatelle

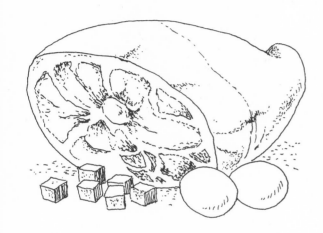

Spaghetti alla meridionale

Spaghetti southern style

1 pound spaghetti
1/2 pound smoked ham, diced
4 eggs

2/3 cup Parmesan cheese, grated
1/3 cup olive oil
salt and pepper

In a large skillet, lightly sauté ham in oil.
In a bowl, beat eggs and add in cheese and salt and pepper.
Cook and strain pasta and add to skillet with ham.
Top with egg mixture and toss briskly over medium heat until egg congeals. Serve immediately.

WINES: Merlot, Bardolino, Chianti classico

ALTERNATE PASTA: Vermicelli, Bucatini, Perciatelli

Linguine con pollo e panna

Linguine with chicken and cream

1 pound linguine
1¼ cups boiled chicken or turkey (boneless,
   skinless), cut into bite-size pieces
3 strips bacon, finely chopped
1 cup light cream

3 tablespoons butter
1 egg, beaten lightly
nutmeg
salt and black pepper

Linguine and sauce should be completed simultaneously.
Melt butter in a large skillet capable of holding the pasta.
Sauté the bacon lightly for a few minutes, then add chicken. Reduce heat to low.
Pour in cream and season with salt, pepper, and nutmeg. Mix gently.
Add linguine cooked al dente and mix thoroughly.
Remove from heat and thoroughly blend in the beaten egg.
This dish should be served hot, so reheat gently if necessary.
Top off each portion with a pinch of nutmeg.

WINES: Cabernet, Pinot nero, Refosco

ALTERNATE PASTA: Spaghetti, Vermicelli

Bucatini allo zafferano

Bucatini with saffron

1 pound bucatini
1/4 pound prosciutto, finely chopped
4 tablespoons Parmesan cheese, grated
3/4 cup light cream

1 tablespoon parsley, finely chopped
2 uncooked egg yolks
1 hard-boiled egg yolk, grated
1/4 teaspoon saffron

Heat cream in a medium pan and blend in cheese.
In separate bowl mix prosciutto, saffron, and a tablespoon of water, then add mixture to sauce pan.
Remove from heat and briskly stir in 2 uncooked egg yolks.
Dress pasta with sauce and top with parsley and grated hard-boiled yolk.

WINES: Frascati, Tocai, Rosé

ALTERNATE PASTA: Vermicelli, Perciatelli

Spaghetti ai fegatini

Spaghetti with chicken livers

1 pound spaghetti
1 medium onion, finely chopped
2 chicken livers
4 tablespoons butter

1/2 cup dry white wine
2 tablespoons capers
2 anchovie fillets, finely chopped
freshly ground pepper

In a medium skillet, sauté onion in butter until onion begins to turn golden.
Add chicken livers and break them up with a fork while cooking.
After 5 minutes, add wine and simmer for another 2 minutes.
Add capers and anchovies. Cook over low heat for about 5 minutes.
Pour sauce over strained pasta and serve.

WINES: Merlot, Bardolino

ALTERNATE PASTA: Vermicelli, Linguine, Spaghettini

The liver, heart, and gizzards of fowl are know in Italy as "regaglie," a word that comes from the Latin
"regalis," which means "kingly" or, more appropriately, "fit for a king."
They are used in a wide variety of gourmet pasta and rice dishes in Italy.

Rigatoni all'Italiana

Rigatoni Italian style

1 pound rigatoni
1½ cups tomatoes, peeled
1/4 pound chicken livers, chopped
1/4 pound mushrooms, sliced
1/8 pound cooked ham, diced
1 small onion, finely chopped

2/3 cup dry red wine
6 tablespoons butter
1 tablespoon fresh basil, chopped
1/4 cup Parmesan cheese, grated
salt and pepper

In a small skillet, sauté liver in 2 tablespoons butter until firm. Remove liver and chop.
In a large skillet, sauté onions in 2 tablespoons butter until softened.
Add ham and mushrooms and simmer for several minutes.
Use more butter if necessary.
Add in cooked liver and peeled tomatoes, and break up tomatoes while stirring.
Salt and pepper to taste.
Simmer over moderate heat for 10 minutes, and stir occasionally.
Raise heat to high and add the wine.
Stir rapidly for 2−3 minutes, then reduce heat to medium for another 7−8 minutes.
Place cooked pasta in heated serving dish, and garnish with remaining butter and basil.
Top with sauce and grated Parmesan. Mix well.

WINES: Merlot, Bardolino

ALTERNATE PASTA: Sedani, Ziti corti, Penne rigate

Perciatelli con salsiccia

Perciatelli with sausage

1 pound perciatelli
3 sweet sausages, skin removed
1/2 cup dry white wine
1 cup beef broth

3 tablespoons butter
1/3 cup Parmesan cheese, grated
salt and pepper

Melt butter in a medium skillet.
Add sausages, break up with a fork, and cook over moderate heat until done.
Pour in wine and continue cooking until wine has evaporated.
Add broth and cook for an additional 15 minutes. Season with salt and pepper.
Dress pasta cooked al dente with sauce and garnish with Parmesan.

WINES: Cirò rosso, Corvo rosso, Cabernet

ALTERNATE PASTA: Vermicelli, Bucatini, Spaghetti, Rigatoni

Many varieties of sausage are produced throughout Italy, and the product varies greatly from region to region. What all the sausages have in common, however, is that they are all made from fresh pork and are not allowed to season, or age, for any length of time.
In some parts of Italy the most prized sausage is made from boar's meat.

Rigatoni alla norcina

Rigatoni Norcina

1 pound rigatoni
3 sweet sausages, skins removed
2 strips lean bacon, diced
1/2 cup Romano cheese, grated

4 tablespoons olive oil
1/2 cup light cream
pinch of black pepper

In a medium skillet, break up sausage with a fork and sauté sausage and bacon in oil over low flame.
When meat is fully cooked, add cream, pepper, and blend thoroughly.
Cook pasta al dente, strain, and combine with sauce in large bowl.
Top with cheese.

WINES: Bardolino, Merlot, Chianti classico

ALTERNATE PASTA: Ziti corti, Penne rigate

Norcia, a small town in the province of Perugia, is famous for its fine sausages and other pork products. "Norcineria," which means "products from Norcia," is often displayed on signs in specialty stores; the name is synonymous with the best sausages in Italy, and is guaranteed to draw a crowd.

Pennette alla Caterina

Pennette Catherine

1 pound pennette
1/2 pound sausage, skin removed
1 cup light cream
1 cup beef broth
3 tablespoons olive oil

3 tablespoons butter
1 small onion, chopped
1/8 teaspoon saffron
4 tablespoons Parmesan cheese, grated
salt and pepper

In a large skillet, sauté onion in oil and butter.
Add sausage and break up into small pieces with a fork.
When sausage is cooked, add broth and simmer until most of the liquid has evaporated.
In a small bowl, combine cream and saffron. Add mixture to sauce and cook over low flame for 3–4 minutes.
Salt and pepper to taste. Pour sauce over cooked pasta.
Mix well and top with Parmesan.

WINES: Pinot grigio, Tocai

ALTERNATE PASTA: All Penne, Rigatoni

Penne al salame

Penne with salami

1 pound penne
1/2 pound salami, cut in cubes
2 tablespoons butter
1 tablespoon olive oil
2 eggs

1/2 cup dry white wine
4 tablespoons Parmesan cheese, grated
1/4 cup crushed rosemary, or one fresh twig
salt and pepper

In a medium skillet, sauté salami in butter and oil with rosemary.
Add wine and let it evaporate until it reduces by one-half.
Remove fresh rosemary twig, and turn off heat.
In a large bowl, beat 2 eggs, add in Parmesan, and salt and pepper to taste.
Add cooked pasta to egg mixture and quickly toss. Add in the salami and sauce. Mix gently.

WINES: Bardolino, Merlot

ALTERNATE PASTA: All Penne

Fusilli Gustosi

Hearty Fusilli

1 pound fusilli
1/4 pound salami, diced
3/4 cup beef broth
1 small onion, finely chopped
1/4 cup parsley, chopped
1 garlic clove, finely chopped

1/2 stick butter
3 tablespoons olive oil
2 tablespoons tomato paste
1/2 cup Parmesan cheese, grated
salt and pepper

Sauté onion, garlic, and parsley in a large skillet with butter and oil.
When onion and garlic have turned golden, add diced salami and cook for about 5 minutes over medium heat.
In separate bowl, mix broth and tomato paste, and then add to sauce.
Salt and pepper. Simmer for at least 10 minutes.
If sauce becomes too thick, add a little water.
Prepare pasta and mix with sauce and 1/4 cup of Parmesan.
Serve remaining cheese as topping.

WINES: Merlot, Chianti classico, Bardolino

ALTERNATE PASTA: Eliche, Sedani, All Penne

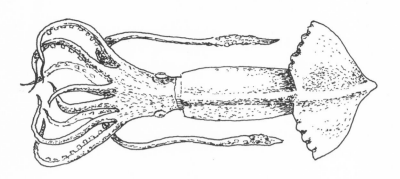

Linguine ai frutti di mare

Linguine with seafood

1 pound linguine
1/2 cup calamaretti (baby squid), cut up
1/2 cup small shrimp, shelled and cut up
12 small hard shell clams, scrubbed
2 cups tomatoes, peeled, cut in pieces
2 garlic cloves

6 tablespoons olive oil
1 tablespoon parsley
1/2 peperoncino (or 2 pinches of hot cayenne pepper)
salt and pepper

Steam clams in a shallow pan. Remove meats, cut in pieces and set aside.
In a medium skillet, sauté garlic and hot pepper in 3 tablespoons of olive oil, and mix in tomatoes.
In a large separate skillet, sauté the calamaretti in remaining olive oil.
When calamaretti are just about done, add in clams and shrimp.
Simmer until fully cooked. Remove pan from heat.
Mix separate sauces together. Season with salt and pepper.
Serve over pasta cooked al dente. Top with parsley.

WINES: Verduzzo, Pinot grigio, Riesling Veneto

ALTERNATE PASTA: Spaghetti, Vermicelli, Trenette

Italy's dramatic coastline boasts many quaint and inspiring scenes, from the ancient fishing villages and mysterious grottos to the majestic seascapes.
Almost every port or village along the coast has a seafood specialty featured in a pasta sauce, but this recipe, with shrimp, clams, and squid, can be found virtually everywhere.

Spaghetti all'appassionata

Spaghetti for a Romantic Evening

1 pound spaghetti	3/4 cup bourbon (whisky)
1 pound fresh shrimp, small size	1 cup tomatoes, peeled, cut in pieces
1 teaspoon freshly ground pepper	1/3 cup Parmesan cheese, grated
2 teaspoons curry powder	1 cup light cream, at room temperature
4 tablespoons olive oil	salt

Boil shrimp for 2 minutes. Remove shells, devein, and rinse.
Place shrimp in large skillet with oil and tomatoes.
Stir in pepper and curry.
Pour bourbon into sauce and continue cooking over low heat. Salt to taste.
Cook pasta, strain, and dress with cream and grated cheese. Mix gently.
Add sauce and serve hot.

WINES: Tocai, Verdicchio

ALTERNATE PASTA: Linguine, Vermicelli

SEAFOOD

102

Penne ai gamberetti

Penne with shrimp

1 pound penne
1 pound small shrimp, boiled and cleaned
1/2 cup dry white wine
1 cup beef broth
6 tablespoons butter

4 eggs (2 whole, 2 yolks)
1/2 cup Parmesan cheese, grated
pinch curry powder
salt

In a large skillet, sauté shrimp in 3 tablespoons of butter, add broth and a dash of salt if needed.
When broth is nearly evaporated, pour in wine.
When the wine has nearly evaporated, add a pinch of curry and continue cooking for 3−5 minutes.
Beat together 2 whole eggs and 2 egg yolks and set aside.
Prepare pasta, strain, and add to pan with sauce. Mix well, and blend in remaining butter.
Add beaten eggs into sauce over medium heat and stir until eggs coagulate and sauce is well blended.
Top with the cheese.

WINES: Pinot grigio, Soave, Tocai

ALTERNATE PASTA: All Penne

Linguine alle vongole saporite

Linguine with tasty clams

1 pound linguine
2 dozen small hard shell clams, steamed and
   shucked
1 cup dry white wine
1/2 cup olive oil
1 dozen scallions, minced

1/2 teaspoon oregano
1/2 cup parsley, minced
1/4 teaspoon thyme
2 garlic cloves, crushed

Mince cooked clam meat.
In a large skillet, sauté the white part of the scallion and garlic in oil for about 5 minutes.
Add clams and parsley and cook for 2 minutes. Reduce heat and add wine, oregano, and thyme.
Simmer for 5–10 minutes. Add salt and pepper to taste.
Pour over pasta cooked al dente. Mix thoroughly.

WINES: Soave, Corvo bianco, Pinot grigio

ALTERNATE PASTA: Trenette, Spaghetti, Vermicelli

*Some Italian cooks sprinkle wine into their skillets as they sauté certain ingredients;
they do this to eliminate fats.
I'm not convinced that fats can be eliminated in this way, but I do know that wine can coax out the hidden
flavors in many sauces. Always use a dry wine, suitable for drinking—never an inexpensive "cooking"
wine—because the finer the wine, the more revealing the taste will be.*

Linguine mari e monti

Linguine of the seas and mountains

1 pound linguine
1/2 pound mushrooms, cleaned and sliced
2½ pounds hard shell clams, cleaned and
  steamed
1 cup tomatoes, peeled, cut in pieces
1 small onion, chopped

1 tablespoon butter
2 tablespoons olive oil
2 tablespoons fresh parsley, chopped
3 fresh basil leaves
salt and pepper

Remove clam meats from shells and place in a large bowl with a little of their juice.
In a large skillet, sauté chopped onion in oil and butter until onion turns golden.
Add mushrooms and cook over medium heat for 3—4 minutes, mixing constantly.
Add tomatoes and season with salt and fresh ground pepper.
Allow the sauce to simmer for about 5—7 minutes.
Add shellfish to the sauce, mix well, season with parsley and let simmer for 2—3 minutes.
Cook pasta and drain. Pour sauce over pasta, mix and serve.
If you prefer, chop cooked shellfish before adding to sauce and leave three or four clams
in the shell as a garnish for each serving.

WINES: Rosé, Chiaretto, Corvo bianco

ALTERNATE PASTA: Spaghetti, Vermicelli, Trenette

The marriage of mushrooms and shellfish has produced some of the greatest pasta sauces.
Mari e monti originated along the coast of southern Italy, particularly from Anzio to the tip of Calabria.
This popular dish is now served throughout the country.

Linguine con salsa di cozze

Linguine in mussel wine sauce

1 pound linguine
3 dozen mussels, steamed and shucked
1 cup dry white wine
1/2 cup olive oil
1 dozen scallions, minced

1/2 cup parsley, minced
1/2 teaspoon oregano
1/4 teaspoon thyme
2 garlic cloves, crushed

Mince 2 dozen mussels, and leave the remaining dozen whole.
In a large skillet, sauté the white part of the scallion and garlic in olive oil for about 5 minutes.
Add minced mussels and parsley and cook 2 minutes over medium heat.
Reduce heat and add wine, oregano, and thyme, and simmer 5−10 minutes.
Salt and pepper to taste. Pour mussel sauce over cooked pasta and toss.
Use the remaining whole mussels to garnish servings.

WINES: Soave, Corvo bianco, Pinot grigio

ALTERNATE PASTA: Spaghetti, Trenette

Mussels are the most popular shellfish in Italy, where nearly every region has a special name for them: mitili, cozze, muscoli, and peoci, to name a few.

Mussels are delicate and sweet, and can be eaten both cooked or raw.
They are prepared in many ways, but wine seems to compliment them best.
Unlike America, where hundreds of thousands of acres of wild mussels lie fallow, the popularity of this shellfish in Italy has forced local fishermen to plant and harvest the mussel crop just like any other scarce commodity.

Linguine dello zar

Linguine of the czar

1 pound linguine
1 cup light cream
2-ounce jar of caviar, red or black

6 tablespoons butter
pinch of freshly ground pepper

Melt 3 tablespoons of butter in a large skillet.
Pour in cream and reduce heat to low, stirring constantly.
Add caviar and mix gently.
Have cooked and strained linguine ready and combine immediately with sauce in same pan.
Mix continuously over low heat until sauce thoroughly coats pasta.
Place in heated serving bowl, add remaining butter, broken in small pieces for easy melting, and season with freshly ground pepper.
If you use artificially colored caviar, the color of the pasta will be affected.

WINES: Prosecco di Valdobbiadene, Pinot grigio, Verdicchio

ALTERNATE PASTA: Trenette, Spaghetti, Vermicelli

Caviar: the food of kings.
The best caviar is the eggs of the sturgeon, a prehistoric fish that can weigh as much as a ton and yield from 20 to 50 pounds of caviar each.
The world's largest producers of caviar are Russia and Iran, where the sturgeon is still relatively abundant, especially in the Caspian Sea.
Good caviar can also come from other fish such as lumpfish and salmon, and can be black, white, red, or grey.

Spaghetti del pirata

Spaghetti of the pirate

1 pound spaghetti
1 small onion, finely chopped
2 cups tomatoes, crushed
1 pint light cream

1 shot cognac
2 ounces smoked salmon, finely chopped
3 tablespoons butter
salt

Sauté onion in butter in a large skillet over low heat.
Add salmon and cook over low heat for 3–4 minutes.
Pour in cognac and simmer until evaporated.
Mix in tomatoes and simmer for 20 minutes. Add cream and mix gently but thoroughly.
Salt to taste. Simmer for 2 minutes.
Pour over cooked and strained pasta. Mix and serve immediately.

WINES: Tocai, Pinot grigio, Soave, Prosecco di Valdobbiadene

ALTERNATE PASTA: Trenette, Linguine, Fettuccine

Tagliolini alla Michelina

Tagliolini Michelina

12 ounces egg-tagliolini
1/2 cup smoked salmon, minced
2 tablespoons cognac
4 tablespoons butter

1 cup medium cream
1 tablespoon Parmesan cheese, grated
1/4 teaspoon black caviar per each serving

Sauté smoked salmon in butter over simmering heat, for about 3 minutes, mixing continuously.
Add 2 tablespoons of cream and when sauce thickens pour in cognac, and mix with a wooden spatula until cognac evaporates.
Add remaining cream and Parmesan cheese.
Mix at moderate heat until sauce becomes creamy.
Pour sauce over pasta and mix rapidly and gently.
Top each individual serving with caviar.

WINES: Velletri bianco, Pinot bianco, Pinot grigio

ALTERNATE PASTA: egg-Tagliatelle

The key to making this sauce is to keep lifting the skillet from the heat as the sauce starts to simmer. This protects the cream as it cooks.
In addition, the sauce should be mixed continuously with a wooden utensil, so that all the delicate ingredients are blended thoroughly and carefully.

Farfalle alla zarina

Faralle of the czarina

1 pound farfalle
5 ounces smoked salmon, finely chopped
2-ounce jar of red caviar

3/4 cup light cream
pinch of freshly ground white pepper

In a large serving bowl, combine salmon and slightly warm cream.
Cook and strain pasta, and pour into bowl containing salmon and cream. Mix.
Top with caviar and season with freshly ground pepper. Toss gently.

WINES: Pinot grigio, Soave, Prosecco di Valdobbiadene

ALTERNATE PASTA: Pennette

Spaghetti alle vongole in bianco

Spaghetti with white clam sauce

1 pound spaghetti
24 hard shell clams, small
6 tablespoons clam juice
1/3 cup olive oil

2 garlic cloves, halved
1/3 cup parsley, finely chopped
1 peperoncino (optional)
salt and pepper

Rinse clams and steam them in a shallow pan until shells open.
Remove clam meats from shells, dice and set aside. Strain and save clam juice.
In a large skillet, sauté garlic in oil, with peperoncino if desired.
Add clam meats, clam juice, one half of the parsley and simmer for a few minutes.
Salt and pepper to taste.
Pour over pasta cooked al dente and top with remaining parsley.

WINES: Corvo bianco, Frascati, Orvieto bianco, Verdicchio

ALTERNATE PASTA: Linguine, Vermicelli, Trenette

This recipe originated in Naples, on the coast.
The combination of clams, olive oil, and garlic are a perennial favorite in villages along the coast,
and are ingredients that are never out of season.

Spaghetti alle vongole col pomodoro

Spaghetti with red clam sauce

1 pound spaghetti
24 hard shell clams, small
6 tablespoons clam juice
1/3 cup olive oil
2 garlic cloves, halved

1/3 cup parsley, finely chopped
1/2 cup tomatoes, peeled, cut in pieces
1 peperoncino (optional)
salt and pepper

Rinse clams and steam them in a shallow pan until shells open.
Remove clam meats from shells, dice and set aside. Strain and save clam juice.
In a large skillet, sauté garlic in oil, with peperoncino if desired; add clam meats, 6 tablespoons of clam juice, one half of the parsley and simmer for a few minutes.
Add tomatoes and simmer for 6—8 minutes. Salt and pepper to taste.
Pour over pasta cooked al dente and top with remaining parsley.

WINES: Corvo bianco, Frascati, Orvieto bianco, Verdicchio

ALTERNATE PASTA: Linguine, Vermicelli, Trenette

Spaghetti alla Carrettiera

Spaghetti of the Teamster

1 pound spaghetti
1/2 pound mushrooms, cleaned and sliced
3⅓ ounces of canned tuna, drained of oil
2 strips bacon, chopped
3 tablespoons beef broth

1 garlic clove
3 tablespoons olive oil
1/4 cup Parmesan cheese, grated
salt and pepper

In a large skillet, sauté garlic in olive oil.
When garlic is golden brown, remove, and add mushrooms and bacon.
Salt and pepper and continue cooking for 5–8 minutes.
While sauce is simmering, cook pasta, strain, and place it in a heated serving bowl.
Add a few tablespoons of hot beef broth to the pasta and mix well.
Add the tuna to the cooking sauce at the last minute and dress pasta with sauce. Mix well.
Garnish individual servings with Parmesan.

WINES: Frascati, Orvieto bianco, Corvo bianco

ALTERNATE PASTA: Spaghettini, Vermicelli, Linguine, Trenette, Bucatini

Fettuccine al tonno con piselli

Fettuccine with tuna and peas

1 pound fettuccine
3⅓ ounces of canned tuna, drained of oil
1/4 pound shelled fresh peas
2 garlic cloves
1 cup tomatoes, peeled, cut in pieces
1/2 cup dry white wine

2 tablespoons butter
2 tablespoons olive oil
1 tablespoon fresh parsley, chopped
2 pinches of crushed hot red pepper
salt and pepper

In a small skillet, sauté peas lightly in butter until cooked, and set aside.
In a large skillet, lightly brown 2 garlic cloves in oil.
When browned, remove the cloves and place tuna in pan.
Break up tuna chunks with fork while cooking.
Add tomatoes, salt, black pepper, and hot pepper. Add peas and mix well.
Pour in the wine and simmer until most of the wine has evaporated, about 5 minutes.
Pour sauce over pasta cooked al dente and top with fresh chopped parsley.

WINES: Tocai, Orvieto bianco, Corvo bianco, Bianco di Custoza

ALTERNATE PASTA: Tagliatelle, Trenette

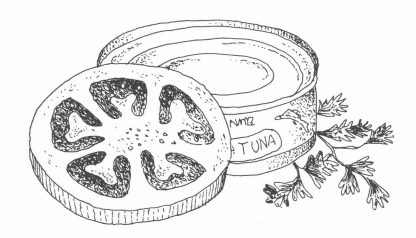

Spaghetti all'isolana

Spaghetti of the islands

1 pound spaghetti	2 garlic cloves, whole
3⅓ ounces of canned tuna, drained of oil	1/2 cup fresh parsley, chopped
2 cups tomatoes, peeled, cut in pieces	3 tablespoons olive oil
1/4 pound mushrooms, cleaned and sliced	salt and pepper

In a large skillet, lightly brown garlic cloves in olive oil.
Add mushrooms and tuna and sauté for a few minutes.
Add parsley and tomatoes. Stir occasionally and cook over medium heat for 15 minutes.
Season with salt and pepper. Pour over pasta cooked al dente.

WINES: Frascati, Orvieto bianco, Tocai

ALTERNATE PASTA: Vermicelli, Trenette, Fettuccine

This recipe originated on the islands off the Italian coast, where both tuna and wild mushrooms are available. Tuna, which is abundant in the Mediterranean, is, like shrimp, considered a delicacy in Italy. The original recipe no doubt called for fresh tuna, but over the years it gave way to the practicality of canned tuna packed in olive oil.

Spaghetti alla Lorena

Spaghetti Lorraine

1 pound spaghetti
10 green olives, cut in quarters
2 teaspoons capers
3⅓ ounces of canned tuna, drained of oil
1/4 cup celery, finely chopped

1 tablespoon onion, finely chopped
2 cups tomatoes, peeled, cut in pieces
1 garlic clove, whole
4 tablespoons olive oil
1 pinch oregano

In a large skillet, sauté celery in oil for 3−4 minutes.
Add onion and garlic and continue cooking until onion has softened.
Add tomatoes. Mix well and simmer for 5 minutes.
Remove garlic, add capers, tuna, oregano and olives, and simmer for 5−6 minutes.
Pour over pasta cooked al dente.

WINES: Orvieto bianco, Tocai, Pinot grigio, Frascati, Corvo bianco

ALTERNATE PASTA: Perciatelli, Bucatini, Vermicelli, Trenette, Fettuccine, Ziti, All Penne

The Eolian Islands, north of Sicily, are a group of seven spectacular islands that are the pride of the Tyrrenian Sea.
In the midst of all this beauty, a true delicacy can be found growing wild between rocks and on stone walls: the caper bush.
Capers are the tiny, aromatic, pungent buds that grow on these bushes. They are a prized export of the Islands.
The climate, marine breezes, and volcanic terrain all contribute to the very special taste and aroma of capers.

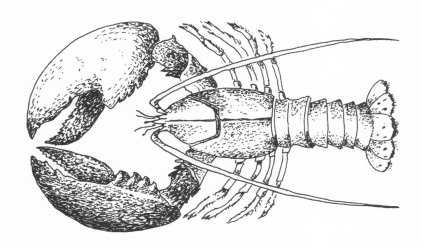

Linguine all'aragosta

Linguine with lobster sauce

1 pound linguine
1/2 pound cooked lobster meat, cut in pieces
1 cup soft melting cheese (i.e. fontina or bel paese), grated
1 cup medium cream

4 tablespoons butter
pinch of tarragon
2 tablespoons parsley, minced
salt and pepper

In a large skillet, blend cream, butter, and cheese over low heat until smooth.
Add lobster meat and season to taste with salt and pepper, and tarragon.
Cook pasta al dente, strain, and place in serving dish. Pour sauce over pasta.
Mix well, and top with parsley.

WINES: Soave, Corvo bianco, Pinot grigio

ALTERNATE PASTA: Trenette, Spaghetti

The beauty of many Italian pasta sauces is that they can be whipped up in minutes. Italians have a saying, "facciamo due spaghetti" which literally means "let's make two spaghetti." However, the saying does not refer to quantity, but to time. Let's make it fast, quickly, in two minutes! The following recipes would certainly fall into this category.

Spaghetti burro e parmigiano

Spaghetti with butter and Parmesan

1 pound spaghetti
6 tablespoons butter in small pieces
2/3 cup Parmesan cheese, grated

4 tablespoons pasta water
freshly ground black pepper

Cook pasta al dente, and place in warm serving bowl.
Mix in butter; when melted, add the hot pasta water and the Parmesan.
Mix thoroughly. Serve with a dusting of freshly ground pepper on each individual serving.

WINES: Frascati, Orvieto bianco, Verdicchio

ALTERNATE PASTA: Linguine, Trenette, Vermicelli

Perhaps the most popular pasta sauce of all, burro e parmigiano is served all over the Italian peninsula.

*Quick and simple, this classic dish is popular as a late night snack, or when friends drop in unexpectedly.
In Caserta, a city near Naples, the natives make a variation of this recipe:
Substitute four tablespoons of the finest virgin olive oil for the butter, and top each serving with a generous helping of cracked black pepper.*

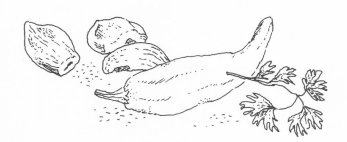

Spaghetti aglio e olio

Spaghetti with garlic and oil

1 pound spaghetti
3 garlic cloves, cut in eighths
6 tablespoons olive oil

1 small peperoncino or crushed hot red
  pepper
1/8 cup parsley, finely chopped

In a medium skillet, place hot pepper and garlic in oil and sauté until the garlic is dark brown but not burnt.
Pour over pasta cooked al dente. Top with fresh parsley.

WINES: Bardolino, Merlot

ALTERNATE PASTA: Linguine, Trenette

This classic recipe is a particular favorite in Naples.
Neapolitans use the word "sciuliarelli," which means "slippery," to describe the preferred consistency of this sauce.
Try not to drench the pasta; use only enough oil to coat the pasta, with little or none left over.
In Abruzzo, there is a nice variation of this recipe: A few minutes before the sauce is ready, stir in one tablespoon of fresh breadcrumbs per person.

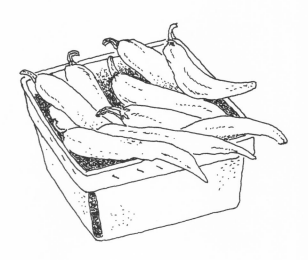

Penne all'arrabbiata
Raging Penne

1 pound penne
4 tablespoons olive oil
2 garlic cloves
2 teaspoons crushed hot red pepper

2 cups tomatoes, peeled and crushed
1/8 cup parsley, chopped
salt

Slice garlic cloves in half. In a large skillet, sauté garlic and pepper until garlic is just light brown, stirring constantly.
Add tomatoes and season with salt. Simmer for another 12–15 minutes.
Sauce should not be watery.
Cook penne al dente, drain, place in serving bowl. Mix in sauce.
Top with fresh chopped parsley.

WINES: Bardolino, Merlot, Chianti classico

ALTERNATE PASTA: All Penne

*This recipe originated in Rome, where cooks like to make this dish as hot as possible.
"Arrabbiata" means "mad" and refers to the abundance of hot red pepper used to "madden" the penne.*

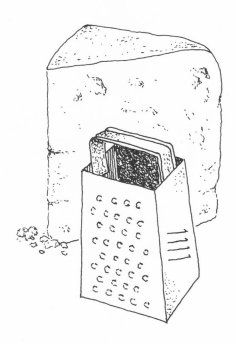

Spaghetti cacio e pepe

Spaghetti with Romano and pepper

1 pound spaghetti
1/3 cup Romano cheese, grated

4 tablespoons of pasta water
black pepper, freshly ground

Cook pasta al dente, strain, saving 3–4 tablespoons of pasta water.
Mix pasta with Romano and the pasta water and top with a dusting of freshly ground pepper.

WINES: Chianti classico, Bardolino, Merlot

ALTERNATE PASTA: Linguine, Vermicelli, Bucatini

This recipe is a rustic and classic pasta sauce that was invented by shephards who once lived in the ancient Roman countryside.
The milk produced from their flocks made the finest pecorino (Romano) cheese,
which is perfectly complimented by crushed black pepper.

Spaghetti della Sila

Spaghetti from Sila

1 pound spaghetti
2 ounces anchovie fillets, chopped
1/2 of a dried peperoncino, cut in small pieces
1 clove garlic

1/3 cup olive oil
1 tablespoon fresh parsley, chopped
salt

Lightly brown garlic in oil. Add hot pepper, anchovies, parsley, and salt to taste. Mix well. Serve over pasta cooked al dente.

WINES: Bianco di Squillace, Cirò Bianco, Corvo bianco

ALTERNATE PASTA: Vermicelli, Bucatini, Perciatelli, Ziti lunghi, All Penne

Sila is a picturesque mountain area in Calabria, which is noted for its many clear lakes and tall evergreen trees. Because of its natural beauty and fine cooking, Sila is popular with tourists, who dine on rich and spicey dishes served in local restaurants.
Sila specializes in pasta sauces made with fresh anchovies, eggplant, hot peppers, cheese, native olive oil, and cherry tomatoes—dishes that have helped make Sila famous for its dining throughout Italy.

In the spring and summer, Italians like to make cold pasta salads. There are no rules for making cold dishes, but Italians seem to prefer wildly colored combinations of vegetables. Cold salads can also be made from vegetables packaged in vinegar or oil for quick preparation.

Ditalini freddi al rosmarino

Ditalini salad with rosemary

1 pound ditalini
2 cups boiled red or white beans
2 ripe tomatoes, cored, cut in small pieces

6 tablespoons olive oil
1 teaspoon rosemary
salt and pepper

Cook pasta al dente, strain, and place in a serving bowl.
Pour in olive oil and mix briskly.
Add beans and tomatoes. Season with salt, pepper, and rosemary.
Refrigerate and serve cold as a salad.

WINES: Rosato Veneto, Chiaretto, Ravello, Soave

ALTERNATE PASTA: Conchiglie, Ditali

Farfalle festive

Festive Farfalle

1 pound farfalle, cooked al dente and strained
1 cup fresh ripe tomatoes, cut in pieces
1 cup fresh mozzarella cheese, diced

6 tablespoons olive oil
2 tablespoons fresh basil, chopped
salt and pepper

Mix all ingredients together. Top with basil.
Refrigerate, and serve cold.

WINES: Prosecco di Valdobbiadene, Soave, Pinot grigio

ALTERNATE PASTA: Conchiglie, Ditali, Farfalline

Spaghetti Arlecchino

Spaghetti of the Harlequin

1 pound spaghetti
1 cup mushrooms, in vinegar, drained
20 black olives, pitted
6½ ounces canned tuna, drained of oil

2 tablespoons fresh basil, chopped
5 tablespoons olive oil
1 orange peel
salt and pepper

In small sauce pan, boil orange peel for one minute, then cut peel into thin strips.
Cook pasta, strain, and combine with olive oil, olives, tuna, mushrooms, and orange peel.
Mix well, and salt and pepper to taste. Top with fresh basil.
Refrigerate and serve cold.

WINES: Frascati, Orvieto bianco, Verdicchio

ALTERNATE PASTA: Vermicelli, Trenette, Linguine

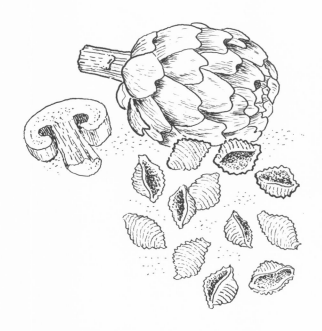

Conchiglie capricciose

Shells caprice

1 pound conchiglie
1 cup mushrooms in oil, drained
8 artichoke hearts, in vinegar, drained
20 small black olives, pitted

5 tablespoons olive oil
2 teaspoons parsley, finely chopped
salt and pepper

Slice mushrooms and artichoke hearts. Cook and strain pasta.
Combine all ingredients in large bowl.
Refrigerate and serve cold.

WINES: Prosecco di Valdobbiadene, Soave, Tocai

ALTERNATE PASTA: Farfalline, Ditali